MW00849051

The Baby Market

The Baby Market

The Case for Adoption Reform

Anne Moody

ROWMAN & LITTLEFIELD
Lanham • Boulder • New York • London

Published by Rowman & Littlefield
An imprint of The Rowman & Littlefield Publishing Group, Inc.
4501 Forbes Boulevard, Suite 200, Lanham, Maryland 20706
www.rowman.com

86-90 Paul Street, London EC2A 4NE

Copyright © 2023 by Anne Moody

All rights reserved. No part of this book may be reproduced in any form or by
any electronic or mechanical means, including information storage and retrieval
systems, without written permission from the publisher, except by a reviewer who
may quote passages in a review.

British Library Cataloguing in Publication Information Available

Library of Congress Cataloging-in-Publication Data
978-1-5381-7471-5 (cloth)
978-1-5381-7472-2 (electronic)

~

Contents

~

Author's Note on Terms

It will be helpful to read this book with an understanding of some of the key participants in adoptions. It will also be helpful to remember that the value of any of these key participants to birth or adoptive parents is dependent upon the individuals involved. Although it is generally true that adoption agencies are staffed by qualified professionals, while adoption facilitators and various types of adoption consultants have no such requirements for training or licensing, it is also true that some facilitators and consultants provide excellent support and advice, while some fully licensed agencies do not. The same can be said for adoption attorneys, most of whom are dedicated professionals but some of whom act in ways that are unprofessional and even un-ethical. Birth and adoptive parents must be cautious and diligent in choosing the people in whom to place their trust—a task that has become increasingly difficult as the ethics of adoption have eroded.

Here are some basic descriptions of the various types of adoption participants:

Birth mother has for many decades been the most commonly used term to describe a woman who has given birth to a child who is subse-quently adopted by someone else. While it is an accurate description, it is sometimes faulted for being dismissively clinical, as is the term "biological mother." Some people are now urging the use of the term "first mother," while others find this dismissive of the adoptive mother, seeming to relegate her to second-place status. For the purposes of this book, I am going to use the term "birth mother" and will make an effort to avoid using it prematurely or presumptively.

I am also going to take liberties with the use of the term **birth father**, primarily by leaving it out most of the time. Although much of what I have to say could be applied equally to the men whose babies are adopted by someone else, the sad truth is that many birth fathers do not take an active role in planning for an adoption. Pretending otherwise is misleading. Consequently, for the sake of both simplicity and accuracy, I have chosen to refer only to the birth mother in most cases. When I describe specific cases in which the birth father was involved, he is included in the story.

Adoption agencies are licensed (and often nonprofit) businesses that are required to uphold established standards of practice and are subject to rigorous governmental oversight. In the state of Washington, where my agency is licensed, this oversight is provided by the Department of Children, Youth and Families (known as the Department of Social and Health Services until 2017.) Every state has an equivalent governmental agency but there are variations regarding what they are called. For example, an agency might be known as the Office of Children and Family Services, the Department of Children and Youth Services, the Department of Human Services, or something similar. Every state is responsible for compliance with federal and state requirements but there may be differences between them in the way child welfare services are operated or delivered.

Agencies typically provide a full range of services for both expectant parents considering adoption and adoptive parents, an essential component of which is counseling both before and after an adoptive placement. Agencies offer the services of adoption professionals who are required to meet licensing standards, including ongoing training to keep their skills current. Agencies work in conjunction with adoption attorneys to assure that legal standards are being upheld.

Adoption facilitation services are businesses whose purpose is to connect prospective birth and adoptive parents, usually through advertising or networking. Facilitators are not required to be licensed or to provide counseling or legal advice to their clients.

Adoptive families who work with facilitators will also need to engage the services of an adoption agency or an adoption attorney, depending on the requirements of the state where the adoption is taking place. Some states prohibit the use of adoption facilitation services altogether.

Adoption attorneys may represent the interests of birth parents, adoptive parents, adoption agencies, and sometimes other adoption professionals. They are responsible for making sure that all applicable laws and standards of practice are upheld, a task that is more complex when the birth and adoptive parents live in different states, as is common these days. There are often two attorneys involved in an adoption: one representing the adoptive parents and one representing the birth parents.

Adoption law centers are most often corporations owned by attorneys who provide services focused on connecting birth and adoptive parents. Like adoption facilitators, they are not subject to the licensing requirements or governmental oversight required of an adoption agency or licensed counselor. They are, of course, required to meet legal standards as established by the bar association in their states.

Adoption consultants are generally individuals who have experience with adoption, either as professionals or as adoptive parents, and feel capable of providing practical advice, emotional support, and other forms of guidance to adoptive parents. Although some may have education and experience as counselors, there is no requirement that they do so, and adoption consultants are generally not required to be licensed.

The terms **private adoption** and **independent adoption** are used interchangeably to refer to any adoption that is not handled by a licensed adoption agency.

Adoption scammers are people who falsely present themselves as considering adoption in order to receive money and/or attention from prospective adoptive parents.

Baby brokers is the term I use for people who orchestrate adoptions for financial gain without regard for the emotional needs of any of the members of the adoption triad (birth parents, adoptive parents, adoptee) They attract pregnant women with promises of financial support and they attract adoptive parents with promises of a quick placement, but no effort is made to provide ethical counsel to either party.

I use the term **adoption counselor** to describe an individual who is a licensed counselor specializing in adoption.

I use the term **adoption professional** to broadly refer to anyone who receives money in exchange for providing adoption services, although the use of the word "professional" is not always accurate or warranted. On occasion I use the term "adoption professional" (in quotes) to describe individuals engaging in what I consider to be very unprofessional behavior.

Acknowledgments

Once again, as was true for *The Children Money Can Buy,* I have borrowed the stories in this book from the people who lived them. While they are all true stories, the details have sometimes been altered to disguise individual people and circumstances. I am enormously grateful to the people who have allowed their personal stories to be used for the greater good of enlightening others and urging adoption reform.

There are many people who have been instrumental in helping me throughout my career. I am grateful to my fellow child welfare workers in Ann Arbor, most specifically Connie Mendenhall, Louann Edwards, Joyce Weigel Sweeney, Mike Dorenkamp, James Johnson, Rocky Gonet, and Mel Kaufman for sharing that life and those stories with me. I also want to thank the World Association of Children and Parents for ten years of experience in working with their dedicated staff and the wonderful families they created through adoption. I owe a special dept of gratitude to Helen McGee and the Options for Pregnancy Program for introducing me to the concept of truly ethical birth parent counseling and open adoption. I want to thank Nita Burks and Dee Axlerod for having the courage to start their own adoption agency and then to turn it over to me and Patti Beasley when the time seemed right. I also want to thank attorneys Mark Demaray, Albert

Lirhus, Rita Bender, Raegan Rasnic, and Dave Anderson for decades of wise and compassionate legal expertise. I especially want to thank my fellow adoption specialists, Ann Lawrence, Dru Martin Groves, and Patti Beasley for their counsel, support, and friendship. And, of course, I want to thank Patti for all the years of partnership as codirectors of Adoption Connections.

There are others who were helpful to me as readers, editors, and advisors, including Nancy Beardsley, Victoria Scott, Anna Quinn, Karen Toler, David and Robin Guterson, Andrew Ward, and Erin Moody. I especially want to thank my sister, Karen Hart, for her wisdom and un-flagging enthusiasm.

I want to thank Suzanne Staszak-Silva, Elaine McGarraugh, and Meghann French for seeing value in this book, for excel-lent advice, and for being a pleasure to work with. I also want to thank Veronica Dove for the cover design. Jaime Quick of C hangeup and Erin Quick of PairTree, have provided invaluable advice and energy in helping me to promote both of my books and sharing my commitment to adoption reform.

Most importantly, I want to thank Fred Moody for all the time and expertise he put into helping me with this book, for showing by example that people can be writers, and for being my perfect partner in life.

~

Introduction

Can This Be Real?

I wrote *The Baby Market* in an attempt to open peoples' eyes to the ethical abuses commonplace in infant adoption today. The book features the experiences of real people, including birth parents, adoptive parents, adoptees, and adoption professionals whom I have worked with in my job as an adoption counselor and codirector of an agency focused on infant adoption. It also includes my own and others' experiences working with people who represented themselves as adoption professionals but behaved in ways that were unprofessional, unethical, and at times even unconscionable. While it is still true that the majority of birth and adoptive families and the professionals they work with manage to create ethical adoptions, it is also irrefutably true that this has become increasingly difficult and that the entire adoption system has been corrupted by the emergence and ascendance of individuals who act as baby brokers. I want the stories in *The Baby Market* to fuel outrage about the ethical deterioration of adoption practice and to fuel efforts to reform what has become a terribly broken system.

Accepted adoption practice has undergone dramatic change over the years, as it became increasingly difficult to adopt an infant at the same time that rates of infertility skyrocketed and economic factors pressured people to delay parenthood. Despite amazing advances in treating infertility, fewer than half of the people seeking this sort of medical intervention succeed in becoming parents. While the success stories are indeed heartening, they are not the norm, leaving adoption the only available route to parenthood for many people.

The combination of factors contributing to the extreme discrepancy between the number of people wanting to adopt a baby and the number of babies available for adoption has created an "anything is fair in (love and war and) adoption" atmosphere. Prospective adoptive parents, including those who uphold the highest ethical standards in every other aspect of their lives, can find themselves on very shaky moral ground in their search for a child to adopt, often without fully understanding how they got there and how to avoid winding up there again as they continue their efforts to adopt a baby. And many adoption professionals find—as I have found—that they need to revise their long-held definition of professional best practices if they want to continue working in this field.

I have worked as an adoption counselor and adoption agency director for almost forty years. My first book, *The Children Money Can Buy: Stories from the Frontlines of Foster Care and Adoption*, was a collection of stories gathered from those years and aimed primarily at providing information and advice for adoptive parents and adoption professionals. The book had a broader purpose as well: I intended it to educate the general public about some of the hard realities inherent in the foster care and adoption systems and to advocate for much-needed change.

In both *The Children Money Can Buy* and *The Baby Market* my intention is to inform the reader about the fact that there really are baby brokers controlling a significant segment of infant adoptions in the United States today. I want people to confront questionable practices in today's adoption system, along with the reality of the huge financial disparity between birth and adoptive parents. I believe that adoptive parents and professionals have a responsibility to recognize that ethical problems exist and that they impact the well-being not only of our own families but of society as a whole.

Adoption is a fascinating subject. Not long after I started working as an adoption counselor, I discovered that people wanted to hear about my job and that even the most routine stories could easily command the room. This was true, in part, because people knew so little about how adoption actually works. They may have been aware of open adoption, usually from media coverage of either a very happy or a very unhappy relationship between birth and adoptive parents. The unhappy relationships, which occasionally resulted in lawsuits and overturned adoptions as well as dramatic coverage on the nightly news and shows like *Dateline*, naturally drew the most public attention. People's understanding of adoption tended to be based mostly on feel-good stories about a baby finding the perfect home and terrifying cautionary tales about a baby being taken away from that perfect home.

One of the things I realized in talking with people about my job was that not only were they unaware of the realities of adoption, but they were often shocked by my stories. I discovered this same shock, and even disbelief, when I wrote *The Children Money Can Buy* and received reviews saying things like, "It doesn't seem possible that all of these things happened to the same person," or simply, "Can these stories be true?"

All the stories in that book, and in this one, are indeed true, and they represent only a small percentage of the people I have worked with, most of whom have stories to tell that are equally remarkable. It seems safe to assume that other adoption professionals have their own collections of compelling stories.

I think it is important that the stories be told, and I am grateful to be in a position to bring them to a wider audience. The people and events I have written about in *The Baby Market* are real or are composites of real people and events. There have been no embellishments for shock value or for the sake of making a stronger argument. In fact, I have actually toned down some of the more upsetting details on the theory that sometimes less is more. I don't want to overwhelm readers with a situation that seems unfixable. Instead, I want to empower them to believe that improvements in the infant adoption system are not only necessary but well within reach.

When writing this type of book, it is imperative to respect the privacy of the people whose stories are being told, and in every case, names and other identifying information have been altered. Most of the stories are told with the full knowledge and cooperation of the people they belong to, but even so, I have opted to preserve confidentiality. This is because it is not yet possible to know what the wishes of the youngest family members—the ones who were adopted as babies—will be and because their wishes and well-being are paramount to all other members of the adoption triad.

CHAPTER ONE

~

The Vagaries of the Marketplace

It must seem obvious that babies should not be bought and sold and that legal adoptions, at least in the United States, would be regulated effectively enough to prevent this sort of transaction. At the same time, there have always been—and continue to be—instances in which birth and adoptive parents and the people who advise them (attorneys, social workers, doctors, ministers, and representatives of both private and state agencies) engage in actions that subvert accepted standards, regulations, and laws governing adoption practice. Historically, black market adoptions and anything resembling them were well hidden, and anyone who engaged in ethically questionable activity was vilified. But, while change has been gradual and largely unacknowledged, I have watched from a front-row seat as what used to be vilified has become normalized. It is now common for some adoption practitioners to use both financial and psychological pressure to coerce women to relinquish babies and to entice hopeful adoptive parents to pay exorbitant fees to adopt a baby. There are numerous shades of gray, many of them quite dark, along the spectrum of acceptable adoption practice today, and the root of the problem, as is often the case, is money.

Infant adoption in this country has a troubled history that includes both a lack of effective governmental regulation and, periodically, egregious and misguided governmental overreach. Despite the abuses of the past, by the mid-twentieth century it was believed, usually correctly, that infant adoption was primarily the domain of well-regulated adoption professionals who were, it was hoped, guided by altruism. This is an assumption I shared for most of my career, but it has become impossible for me to ignore the ethical abuses that now negatively impact the entire adoption system.

Adoption professionals like me can look and feel a lot like baby brokers these days, and it's not a feeling—or a reality—that anyone is happy about. It is, of course, reasonable that agencies, consultants, counselors, attorneys, and other professionals involved in orchestrating adoptions get paid for their time and expertise. And it is true that adoptions have become increasingly complex, both logistically and ethically. Birth and adoptive parents often require and desire a great deal of guidance to help them through the process of relinquishing a baby, adopting a baby, and orchestrating their ongoing relationships with one another in this era of open adoption.

The cost of an adoption has risen so dramatically and unpredictably in the past decade that it has become an unattainable reality for an increasingly large percentage of hopeful adoptive parents. In years past, it was financially feasible for the average middle- or working-class family to adopt a baby. It wasn't easy, but it was possible. I knew many young families who were able to accomplish this dream through some belt-tightening, by taking on a second job for a while, or by taking on some debt. My own youngest child's adoption was funded by the fortuitous demise of my husband's first (failed) business and its sale for almost the exact amount of the adoption fees. I knew another family who joked about how they probably should have given their daughter the middle name Visa, in honor of the company that had made it possible for them to adopt. The cost of an adoption in those days was a far smaller percentage of the average family's income, and a Visa-funded adoption could be paid off over a far shorter period of time.

Like homes, college educations, and everything else, the cost of adoption has skyrocketed in the past two decades, out of all proportion to increases in income. But unlike houses and college educations, most adoptions must be paid for up front. While it is possible for a family to get a bank loan or another form of assistance to help pay for an adoption, it's a lot harder to get a loan (or pay it back) when the family is already struggling with student loan debt, medical bills (from unsuccessful and often uninsured infertility treatment), and/or exorbitant housing costs, all of which plague many prospective adoptive parents.

To make matters even more stressful, there is the time factor to be considered. The majority of the adoptive parents I now work with are in their forties, at least a decade older than the people I worked with during the first half of my career. These are people who delayed starting their families until their mid- to late thirties, feeling this was the responsible course of action. They wanted to achieve a level of career and financial security that would allow at least one of them to take an extended parental leave to devote themselves to raising children when the time came. Instead, they were faced with infertility and uncertainty, along with years of medical treatments and the accompanying bills. Working through the grief surrounding infertility and often pregnancy loss is a heavy and ongoing burden for many, but eventually these people felt able to look toward a hopeful future in which they could become parents through adoption. Then they were confronted with the enormous and often unpredictable cost of adoption and the corresponding need to amass an enormous and often unpredictable amount of money before they were deemed too old to be the parents of a baby.

This is the basic background story for many of the families who contact me. By the time I meet them, they have scraped together the money for an adoption, but they have run out of time. Consequently, they find themselves wanting/needing to cast aside the caution and good sense that would normally guide them through big decisions and expenditures. Some of these people decide they are willing to do whatever it takes financially to adopt a baby, and this makes them perfect targets for exploitation. Sadly, various unethical middlemen are eager to exploit them.

Another sad thing is that these families are actually the fortunate ones. For the most part, they come from backgrounds of privilege, and despite the considerable hardships they have faced, they will probably prevail in the end. They are the ones who will succeed in bringing a child into their families. Most of them are white, with college educations, satisfying careers, access to good medical care and secure housing, and reliable extended family ties to give them financial and emotional support when needed. They are good and deserving people, and I am overjoyed when they are able to adopt. But there are also lots of people who aren't so fortunate and who, despite being just as good and deserving, will never have the opportunity to become parents. These are people I will probably never hear from because they have already given up on the idea that they could ever afford to adopt a child.

Still, some of them try. I periodically get calls from women who tell me that they and their husbands have just decided that they want to adopt "our first baby." Usually the caller says something about how she knows that there are babies who need homes and, since she and her husband are perfectly comfortable with the idea, they figured they'd start their family by adopting. The fact that the caller thinks there are many babies who need homes lets me know that I should settle in for a long conversation. We talk for a while, and she reveals that they have been married for a number of years and have been trying to have children for most of that time. I'm sure there are exceptions, but it is extremely rare for people to deliberately choose infant adoption, with all its expense and uncertainty, when they are able to give birth to a baby. So I assume there must be more to the story but that it can't be told in a single telephone conversation.

The caller tells me she has heard that the first thing adoptive parents need is a home study, and she wants to schedule an appointment with me to get started on that. I ask her if she and her husband have decided what type of adoption (private, agency, facilitator, etc.) they will be pursuing and explain that this will influence what type of home study they need. For example, some agencies require a particular format for home studies, some agencies will only use home studies written by their own counselors, and there may be other rules that I know nothing about. I tell her that I want to make sure the home study I write will ultimately be useful to them.

Although I don't know much else about her, I'm already pretty sure that she is not one of the highly educated and professionally successful women who are my typical clients these days and who have almost always done exhaustive research before I hear from them. Instead, it is apparent that this woman knows very little about adoption, including the fact that adopting a baby is likely to be an extremely difficult and expensive process, and I now have the sad task of breaking this news to her.

It is heartbreaking. The only thing that separates this woman from my usual clients is money and the privileges it brings. Of course, money—and the lack of it—creates inequities in many areas of life, but the fundamental ability to raise a family is not usually one of them. Rich and privileged people have no advantage over other people when it comes to procreation, but they certainly do when it comes to adoption. Rich and privileged people also have no advantage over other people when it comes to being able to be loving and devoted parents. They may be able to provide certain advantages, but these do not in themselves contribute to the creation of happier children or families.

It makes sense that the adoption system, and birth parents themselves, would favor adoptive families who can provide a level of financial security that is sufficient to meet the child's needs for care and stability. But our society has always recognized that children and families can thrive within a wide range of socioeconomic conditions. The struggling working-class family with few extras but an abundance of love is one of our favorite stereotypes, as is the rich family with every material advantage but no warmth. We like to believe that children from the first sort of family grow up to be hardworking, responsible, appreciative, and loving, while children who are financially privileged are at risk of becoming lazy, entitled, selfish, and ungrateful. Anyone who works with birth mothers comes to realize that contrary to what might be expected, most of them do not choose adoptive families based on displays of material wealth. They are more likely to be drawn to families who feel familiar and comfortable.

I don't ask the prospective adoptive mother anything about her own financial situation. I just present, as gently as I possibly can, information about the financial realities of adoption. I assume that she and I, neither of whom are wealthy, will feel equally outraged by how expensive it is to adopt a baby. Usually, though, she responds not with outrage but with solemn dismay, probably reserving her outrage for a time when she feels safe expressing it. After that there are lags in the conversation while she comes to grips with what I have said and recalculates how best to proceed.

I ask her if she has considered working with the foster care system, urge her to contact the Department of Children, Youth and Families, and refer her to various online sources of information about adoption. I also give her the name of one of the attorneys I work with who offers a free initial consultation at which she could learn a lot about the logistics and legalities of a private adoption. We've usually talked for thirty minutes or more by this point and I end the conversation by saying that I will go ahead and send her all the information she'll need in case she decides to have me do the home study. I tell her that I wish infant adoption wasn't so expensive, she thanks me for my time, and I wish her well. Most of the time I don't hear back from these women. I would love to believe that they have successfully connected with DCYF and will be pursuing adoption of a child from the foster care system, but I suspect that's rarely the case.

There are many inequities in our society, but this one feels especially immoral. We have allowed money to be the final arbiter of who gets to adopt an infant and who doesn't. We have allowed this even though we know there is no correlation between high income and successful parenting and that this approach will prevent an abundance of extremely well-qualified potential parents from having children. I understand that this has happened because there are far fewer babies available for adoption than there are families hoping to adopt them. On balance, it is absolutely wonderful that every baby is so very wanted. But it is not wonderful that this has created a situation in which many babies essentially go to the highest bidders.

Let me further explain my concern about the current state of adoption by telling you about five of the families I worked with recently, providing them with a home study and counseling as they pursued infant adoption. These families include four white couples, one of them a gay couple, and a Black single mother who had, years earlier, adopted a special-needs baby through the state foster-to-adopt program. Because of the years of stress and uncertainty she had encountered in finalizing her first adoption, she was unwilling to pursue another foster-to-adopt placement and risk having her older child experience similar stress about the possibility of losing her beloved sibling if the state ultimately decided the baby should be returned to his or her parents.

Three of these families worked with a traditional adoption agency and two worked with adoption facilitators to complete private adoptions. The families waited between seven months and two years for their children, and each baby suffered prenatal drug exposure, with varying degrees of impact on their well-being at birth. There were other health issues as well, including gestational diabetes, birth mothers testing positive for HIV and hepatitis B, low birth weight, and a traumatic birth resulting in the baby being given an APGAR score of 1 and immediately placed on a ventilator. The APGAR test indicates, on a scale from 1 to 10, how well a baby is doing at one minute and five minutes after birth. This baby had just barely survived.

In each of these cases, the hospital was unlikely to have released the baby to his or her mother. If an adoption hadn't been planned, child protective services (CPS) would most likely have placed the baby in a foster home, and many months, if not years, would pass while the state worked to determine the best outcome for the child. Some of these babies required intensive care and many weeks of hospitalization, while others were released from the hospital after only a few days. Although it is too soon to make definitive statements about their long-term health and development, these babies are currently in good health and appear to be developing normally. It is nothing less than miraculous that all of them found their way into wonderful families in which they are loved and treasured and will be given every opportunity to thrive.

All these adoptions were extremely expensive, and all but one of the birth mothers seem to have resumed their lives of hardship and dysfunction. It's only been a few months since that woman's baby was born, however, and her newfound stability is tenuous, despite the ongoing efforts of the agency and continued financial and emotional support from the adoptive parents.

I am particularly aware of how unethical things have become when I am contacted by an adoption professional who is looking for a family for what is called a "hard-to-place" baby, a description that often means the expectant mother has mental health or substance abuse issues. There is still an abundance of prospective adoptive parents who are eager to adopt these babies, but it might take just a little extra effort on the part of the adoption professional to locate one of them. In these cases, that extra effort usually amounts to sending emails to other adoption professionals (like me) in hopes that we are working with a family who would be interested in adopting the baby and paying whatever fees are being requested.

The expectant mother has often contacted the adoption professional in response to an advertisement offering to pay her living expenses. She wants help finding a family for the baby and she needs financial assistance for herself. In turn, the adoption professional is looking for an adoptive family who will provide living expenses for the mother along with whatever fee the adoption professional is charging. The search for a family generally stops when the first acceptable one agrees to send money and the woman agrees to "choose" them. This approach toward helping a woman find "the perfect family" for her baby would be laughable were it not so tragic and enraging.

My outrage comes from the knowledge that this is basically a financial transaction. No one is really looking out for the best interest of this baby—something that becomes particularly evident with interracial placements. As the mother of an adopted child of a different race, I am obviously a proponent of interracial adoption. But I also believe that whenever possible, it is preferable for children to be placed in same-race adoptive families. These positions are not contradictory, just as it is not contradictory for me to believe in the rightness of my own family and the many other interracial families I know while still working hard to find same-race families for babies.

When I am contacted by an adoption professional who is looking for a family for a "hard-to-place" Black baby, for example, I know they are not really looking for the perfect family for that baby. They are simply looking for a family who meets the basic requirements for adoption and will pay the fee. And they are essentially bribing the expectant mother (with the promise of paying her living expenses) to do the same. No one is even pretending to do otherwise. There are all sorts of wonderful families (same race and different race) who would like to adopt this child, but the baby's parental options are limited by the financial desires of the adoption professional who is offering the baby's mother money via the first available adoptive family. That first family may turn out to be a wonderful family for the child, but that would simply be good luck rather than the result of any careful attention to the child's best interest.

Given the expectation of openness in modern adoption, it has become more important than ever for birth and adoptive families to be given the opportunity to get to know one another prior to the adoption. If these people are going to have ongoing roles in each other's lives, they need to be able to establish relationships that are based on honesty and respect as well as a mutual concern for the well-being of the child. Instead, the current approach to adoption too often supports what I call "baby brokering," and I have sadly observed what appears to be a growing disconnect between some birth and adoptive parents. I believe that the exchange of ever-larger sums of money has acted to erode their confidence in one another. I also believe that all pregnant women who are struggling financially should receive whatever assistance is necessary to ensure that they and their babies are safe and healthy. But this assistance should come from the government or another neutral entity, not from individuals who are hoping to adopt the babies, and should be in no way tied to an adoption agreement. Enticing women to "consider adoption" (or pretend to be doing so) in exchange for money is clearly coercive and sets the stage for exploitation of both birth and adoptive parents.

We now seem to be in what one adoptive parent I worked with called "the Wild West of adoption," where might (in this case, money instead of guns) makes right. As in the Wild West, the law is hard to find, and those who successfully get what they want are likely to be the ones who have taken it into their own hands.

That's what happens when we let the marketplace control adoption. And it is wrong.

CHAPTER TWO

~

Owen and Kira

An Adoptive Family's Story

Owen and Kira did their student teaching at the same high school. The twenty-two-year-olds both thought they were nowhere near ready to settle down with anyone until they met each other and realized they couldn't imagine ever being apart. The third time they went out alone together, the conversation was mostly about how much they both wanted to have children someday. By date number four it seemed to be mutually understood that they would have those kids together. They got married when they were twenty-four, after a couple years of talking and planning and agreeing on just how they wanted to live their lives.

Owen and Kira were always in agreement about their long-term plans: settling down in the town where they grew up, buying their own home, saving enough money so that Kira could stay home for at least a few years when they had children. It wasn't going to be easy on teachers' salaries, but they were frugal people, highly motivated to achieve their goals, and had a lot of years ahead of them. They were practical, hardworking, and quite willing to make sacrifices.

Owen and Kira were also very young when they got married, and they wanted some adventure before settling down. So they decided to accept jobs at an international school in Italy. Those were wonderful years, and Owen and Kira ended up teaching there for six years instead of the three they had planned. They also ended up being able to save

14

quite a bit of money, even while they spent all the school holidays exploring Europe. It was hard to leave their jobs, where they were appreciated and well-liked by the students and fellow staff members, but by the time they were thirty, Owen and Kira felt ready for the next stage of life.

They moved back to their hometown and got jobs at different high schools. The real estate market had changed dramatically during the years they were gone, and Owen and Kira were disappointed to realize that although they had saved what they thought would be a sizable down payment, it wasn't going to be enough to buy them the house they had imagined. They hadn't imagined anything elaborate, but they weren't willing to compromise on living in what they considered to be a safe neighborhood with good schools. They decided to live with Kira's parents for a while and save every penny they possibly could.

Two years later, Owen and Kira were able to buy a small house in the district where Owen taught. Although it was a long commute from Kira's school, they were looking ahead to the time when she would be at home with children and figured it would be better if they lived near Owen's school. When it was time for Kira to return to teaching, they hoped she would be able to find a job in that district as well. They were thrilled to became homeowners at age thirty-two and were eagerly looking forward to the next step in their carefully laid plan: having children.

This step didn't go as anticipated. It was hard when the months passed by without a pregnancy, but they told themselves this was perfectly normal. Kira had always had irregular periods, but none of her doctors had ever seemed concerned. Her current doctor assured her that at her age there was nothing to worry about, but if she still wasn't pregnant after a year, they might consider further testing. So after a year Owen and Kira sought help from a clinic specializing in infertility and underwent various tests and treatments for another year. No specific problem was found, which also meant there was no specific treatment indicated, but they still tried various things with no success and increasing despair. They tried fertility drugs, which were hard on Kira physically and psychologically, and they tried five rounds of artificial insemination, which were hard on both of them emotionally each time they failed to produce a pregnancy. These things were also hard on Owen and Kira financially because almost none of these procedures were covered by their insurance.

When they were thirty-six, Owen and Kira decided to take a different approach. They were practical and realistic people, and while they weren't giving up on the idea of having a child by birth, they revised their plan to include adopting their first child. They had hoped to have two children, three years apart, by the time they were forty, so from now on everything really needed to go according to plan.

Owen and Kira approached adoption with their usual energy and optimism but quickly found themselves confused and frustrated. They read lots of books and articles on infant adoption, but it almost felt as if the more research they did, the more confused they became. There were all sorts of people, including both professionals and other adoptive parents, who were eager to offer information and advice, but it often conflicted, leaving Owen and Kira wondering what was true and who they could trust. For example, there was no consensus about the pros and cons of using an adoption agency or a facilitation service, and there was definitely no agreement about the "best" way to adopt. In fact, there was no shortage of people telling horror stories about their experiences, no matter which approach they had taken. Of course, there were also lots of feel-good stories from happy families after they had successfully adopted, but even these were often tempered by warnings about the hardships the adoptive parents had experienced prior to finally finding their child. It was daunting and discouraging, to say the least.

Owen and Kira struggled with the uncertainty of the adoption process and were shocked to discover how hard it was to get what they felt was reliable, let alone reassuring, information about the things that most concerned them. They wanted someone to tell them they would be able to adopt a child who was in good health, and it was hard for them to learn that adopted children (like all children) came with no guarantees of continued good health. They wanted someone to guarantee that nothing could go wrong legally, and it was hard to learn that even the most well established and highly respected agencies and attorneys couldn't make this promise. They also wanted someone to be able to tell them what an adoption would cost, and it was hard to hear how unpredictable that amount could be. The only "assurances" all their research produced seemed to be from people who were urging them to send money immediately in order not to miss out on a time-limited opportunity. Fortunately, Owen and Kira were wise enough to recognize that such assurances were false.

The best result from all their online research was that it connected Owen and Kira with other adoptive parents who generously shared their experiences and advice. Owen and Kira's research also gave them information about a local adoptive parent support group, and Kira contacted some of the women involved. She discovered that a few of them had adopted their children through a local attorney who specialized in adoption. All the children were thriving and none of their adoptions had involved scary and expensive legal complications. The cost of their adoptions had varied widely because some of the families had paid for living expenses for their child's birth mother and others had not. Although the upper end was about twice as high as Owen and Kira had expected, they could come up with the money if they had to, even if it meant taking on a loan or a second mortgage.

Owen and Kira finally found the reassurance they were seeking when they met with the attorney the other parents had recommended. His manner was calm and easygoing, and he was a long-standing member of the American Academy of Adoption Attorneys, an organization of experienced and highly respected adoption attorneys. He didn't sugarcoat the process or make promises about the health of the baby, but Owen and Kira were now savvy enough about adoption to understand and appreciate his honesty. They knew there would be risks and that becoming parents, whether by birth or adoption, requires a leap of faith. Owen and Kira felt ready to take that leap with the assistance of a man they felt they could trust to guide them safely.

They eagerly started the home study process and carefully prepared a profile of pictures and information about themselves for the attorney to show to prospective birth parents. He had explained to them that they would also need to post their profile on at least one adoption website, because it was rare for birth parents to contact him directly. That only happened a handful of times each year, but, incredibly, it happened for Owen and Kira. They had just posted their online profile and received responses from a couple of people who had then promptly disappeared, when the attorney called them with exciting news. A pregnant girl had come into his office that week wanting to see profiles. When he asked her what she was looking for in an adoptive family, the only thing she said was that it would be nice if one of them was a teacher. She had looked at Owen and Kira's profile and now wanted to meet them. The girl, Lindy, was expecting a baby girl in ten weeks.

A few days later, Owen and Kira met with Lindy and her foster mother in the attorney's office. He had told them that Lindy was sixteen, had been in foster homes for the past five years, was very quiet, and apparently hadn't realized (or at least hadn't acknowledged) that she was pregnant until almost the seventh month. Whatever uncharitable images Owen and Kira had formed about someone who could be six months pregnant without knowing it vanished as soon as they saw Lindy. She was tall and slim and carried herself with a calm grace. Even knowing she was pregnant, it was hard to discern much of a baby bump. Lindy was clearly shy, and the situation made Owen and Kira feel shy as well, so the foster mother and the attorney did most of the talking for a while. Owen and Kira tried to think of things to say that would make Lindy choose them, but it was hard not to just stare at her in amazement and imagine the beautiful baby who would be born in a few months.

When the meeting in the office ended, the attorney suggested that the rest of them might like to continue talking in a coffee shop down the street. By the time they were seated at a small table and the foster mother had excused herself to make a call, Owen and Kira had regained their normal social skills. Lindy was still quiet, but she answered their questions thoughtfully and even had some questions of her own for them. She was polite and obviously bright, but she was also extremely reserved and seemed sort of detached—or, more likely, depressed. It was impossible to tell what she was thinking, and Owen and Kira were surprised and thrilled when the attorney called the next day to say that Lindy had chosen them.

The attorney explained that although there was some uncertainty with regard to the father of the baby, overall this was a good situation. Lindy and her caseworker both seemed certain that adoption was the best choice, and since Lindy was a minor, a guardian ad litem would be appointed to protect her interests. But when the attorney contacted Matt, the man Lindy said was the father, he responded that he wasn't the only one who could be the father and he wasn't going to sign any papers. The attorney told Matt that he understood his concerns, gave him the names of several attorneys he could consult, and told him that the adoptive parents would be responsible for any legal fees. That all seemed hopeful, but there was no follow-up on Matt's part, and three weeks later Lindy told the attorney she had heard that Matt had moved out of state. This complicated things legally, since Matt's legal rights couldn't be terminated without his voluntary relinquishment until the baby was about a month old. Owen and Kira would have to agree to an "at-risk placement," meaning that they would need to take custody of the baby before she was legally free for adoption. Neither Lindy's nor Matt's rights would have been terminated, and Owen and Kira would have to give up the baby if either parent changed their mind about the adoption during that month.

This was exactly the sort of situation Owen and Kira had said they didn't want to get involved in, but here they were anyway. The attorney told them he couldn't make any promises, but that it didn't seem as though Matt's disappearance was based on his objection to an adoption. It was more likely to be based on his objection to being held responsible for Lindy's pregnancy and wishing to avoid long-term financial responsibility for the child if Lindy didn't follow through with an adoption. Matt, who Lindy thought was twenty-one, may also have been feeling anxious about the legal ramifications of the age difference between himself and Lindy. It seemed pretty safe to say that Matt's departure didn't seem like the response of someone who wanted to be a parent.

Owen and Kira decided that they wouldn't let themselves worry about the possible risks of Matt's disappearance, and the remaining weeks flew by in happy preparation. Kira's friends had agreed to hold off on an official baby shower until after the baby was born, but that didn't stop them from "showering" her and Owen with all sorts of wonderful hand-me-downs. The baby's room and furniture were freshly painted and the closet, drawers, and shelves filled with clothing, toys, books, and bedding, with friends and family eagerly waiting to provide even more.

Kira was thrilled when Lindy asked if she wanted to come to her doctor's appointments. The foster mother was there as well, but she was good about giving Lindy and Kira time alone together. Lindy was always extremely considerate about answering the questions Kira had about how she was feeling and how the baby was doing. Still, Lindy was reserved, and Kira felt cautious with her. One day while they were waiting in the doctor's examination room, Kira surprised them both by reaching out and resting her hand on Lindy's stomach. They watched as the baby moved under Kira's hand and then they burst into laughter together. Lindy had told them that she was still thinking about what would be best with regard to staying in contact after the adoption, but Owen and Kira had already decided that they hoped this lovely, thoughtful person would continue to be part of their lives.

Baby Rose was born on a Monday morning: eight pounds, six ounces, with light brown hair and enormous, calm eyes, just like Lindy's. Owen and Kira had been poised outside the delivery room door, at Lindy's request, and were called into the room a few minutes after the birth. It was love and awe and elation and gratitude and a million other emotions at first sight. Rose was initially taken to the newborn nursery, also at Lindy's request, with Owen and Kira never leaving her side. But that afternoon, as Rose slept, Kira peeked into Lindy's room and saw that she was awake and alone, and there was a quick change of plans. Soon everyone was together in Lindy's room, oohing and ahhing over Rose, and that evening the new grandparents and an aunt and uncle came to meet her and Lindy.

Although it was clearly a time of celebration for the adoptive family, they were not insensitive to Lindy's feelings. She was, as she always had been, quiet and uncomplaining, but they knew her outward demeanor couldn't possibly reflect all her emotions. Lindy didn't want to be left alone with Rose, and none of them wanted Rose to be left in the nursery, so Owen and Kira took turns going home to sleep for a few hours that night. The rest of the time they spent in Lindy's room at the hospital, just staring at Rose or at each other in ecstatic disbelief.

The next day the hospital social worker met with Lindy to confirm that she was not being coerced into the adoption, and by late afternoon, both Lindy and Rose were ready for discharge. Everyone was just waiting for the attorney to show up with the legal paperwork allowing Rose to go home with her new parents.

But that's not what happened. Instead the attorney showed up with the devastating news that the father had resurfaced and was asking for paternity testing. If the baby was his, then his parents wanted her.

And that is what happened.

The legal system had allowed Matt to take zero responsibility during the pregnancy and swoop in after the baby was born to overturn all of Lindy's wishes and all of Owen and Kira's careful planning. It wasn't as though Matt's rights hadn't been respected all along the way. He had consistently ignored the attorney's efforts to involve him and then disappeared. It was especially painful to know that Matt had this immense power over Lindy and the baby (and Owen and Kira) even though he had no intention of raising his child. At first it felt to Owen and Kira that Matt had little interest in the baby but was just hanging on to what was his. Perhaps that wasn't quite fair to Matt and his family, though, and when Owen and Kira realized that Matt's parents weren't that much older than they were themselves, it made complete sense that they would want to raise their granddaughter.

It made sense, but it didn't lessen the pain of losing Rose. Owen and Kira could no longer bear to look at the beautiful but empty nursery, so Kira's mother and some friends came over and packed everything into boxes and stored them in the garage. Of course, the boxes reminded them of Rose every time they pulled into the garage, but it wasn't as though they could forget her anyway. They needed time to grieve, but they told the attorney they were ready to try again and reactivated their webpage.

The first contact through the website was from a woman who said she was seven months pregnant and told them she "just knew right off when I saw your pictures that you were going to be the parents of this baby." She told them that she had to do an adoption because babies should have a mom and a dad, and her boyfriend, the father of the baby, had been in a motorcycle accident last month and was probably going to die. Kira responded with shock and sympathy. Over the next two weeks, the woman called every few days, her stories becoming increasingly alarming, including detailed accounts of ritualistic childhood sexual abuse at the hands of a church elder. Kira began to dread hearing the phone ring. Owen thought she should just put an end to the calls and tell the woman that they had been chosen by someone else, but Kira wasn't ready to give up on the possibility of adopting this baby. After enduring what seemed like countless hours of listening to horrible stories, Kira's patience finally began to wane and she told the woman that she had to take the next step and contact their attorney if they were to keep talking. The woman called a few more times after that, but when Kira repeated her request about calling the attorney, there was silence. The woman did not call again, nor did she answer or return calls. Kira reached out to her through email shortly before the baby was due to be born and received a reply saying that the boyfriend had been taken off life support and she had decided to keep the baby "because it's all I have to remember him by."

Owen never even hinted at an "I told you so," but Kira berated herself for having wasted so much time and emotion on what, in retrospect, was clearly a scam. Over the next few months there were a few more calls from women, but they never called a second time, even after saying that they would. Again Kira berated herself. Was her voice betraying the caution and suspicion and desperation she now felt? Even worse was a five-month period with no contacts at all, not even scams. Intellectually Owen and Kira knew that adoption could take a long time, but it felt as though they had reached a complete standstill.

They began to reconsider signing up with an agency but were discouraged by the fees, which seemed impossibly high. They had seen ads from an attorney in another state who, for $200, would present a family's profile to an expectant mother. It seemed worth the relatively small fee to try this method. After all, it had been an attorney who connected them with Lindy. Maybe there would be another pregnant woman considering adoption who wanted a couple of teachers for her baby. Owen and Kira sent off the money, but the woman chose someone else. Then they sent money two more times, and never heard back, one way or the other, from the attorney. Six hundred dollars felt like a lot to spend on nothing, the same way it felt when they spent another $800 to renew their online advertising, which continued to yield nothing.

Over the next year and a half they did get a few calls from women who were asking for money, always needing it be sent immediately. When Owen or Kira explained that any financial arrangements would have to go through their attorney, these women would disappear. A couple of times the attorney sent their profile to women who had come into his office, but they always ended up choosing someone else.

Finally, one day Owen and Kira were contacted by a woman who said she was an adoption facilitator and had seen their profile online.

She was working with an expectant mother who was due in two weeks and wondered if they would be interested in finding out more about the situation. Of course they would! The counselor told them that the woman, Darcy, had been working with another adoptive family but that there had been some sort of disagreement and Darcy no longer wanted to place her baby with them. The facilitator felt it was all an unfortunate and very badly timed misunderstanding, but nevertheless she needed to find Darcy a new family at the eleventh hour.

The facilitator explained that the way the finances worked was that the adoptive family was expected to pay one half of the fee if they were matched with Darcy, meaning that she chose them and they all wanted to go ahead with the adoption. The second half of the fee would be due before the placement of the baby. Owen and Kira said that they would be interested in getting more information about Darcy, and a few minutes later they received the following:

Birth Mother: Darcy
Age: 37
Race: Caucasian
Birth Father: Unknown
Race: Caucasian or African American
Health: ADHD, some depression (possibly situational), prenatal care beginning in the seventh month. No current concerns.
Alcohol: Occasional use prior to knowing she was pregnant (fifth month)
Drugs: Occasional use of marijuana and cocaine prior to the fifth month
Other children: Sixteen-year-old son and fourteen-year-old daughter live with ex-husband. Nine-year-old daughter (different father) lives with paternal grandmother.
Asking for living expenses of $900 per month. Total cost of the adoption, including legal fees, estimated at about $32,000.

It wasn't exactly reassuring information, except in two very important ways. It seemed unlikely that Darcy would change her mind and decide to raise this child since she wasn't raising any of her other children. It also seemed unlikely that a father who was "unknown" would show up and claim the baby as his. The other factor that influenced Owen and Kira to go ahead was that the baby was due so soon. As the facilitator had explained it, they would only be responsible for two months of living expenses, and if the adoption fell through for any reason, they could either be refunded half the facilitation fee or they could apply the entire fee to another adoption through this facilitator.

Owen and Kira wanted to talk with Darcy but were told that after her experience with the first family, she didn't want to talk to anyone else. Owen and Kira also wanted to have some time to talk with their doctor about the risks of prenatal drug and alcohol exposure. The facilitator encouraged them to get this information but also told them that since it was so late in Darcy's pregnancy, she would need their answer within twenty-four hours. Owen and Kira managed to reach their doctor later that day, but she was understandably noncommittal about making any sort of recommendation. She did refer them to some websites on the subject, which were frankly terrifying.

Owen wanted to say no at that point, but Kira kept researching and found information aimed specifically at adoptive parents dealing with the issue of prenatal drug and alcohol exposure. This time what they read was far more encouraging, as parents told their own stories of having adopted babies who had been exposed to various drugs in utero. As Kira interpreted their stories, it seemed as though the worst that was likely to happen was that the baby would go through withdrawal for a week or so and then would be fine. Owen was far more skeptical, but he eventually agreed with Kira that they could always say no if there was a problem with the baby. If that happened the facilitator would allow them to apply part of their fee to the next situation that came along. Owen reasoned that at worst, they would have to start all over, but this time with a facilitator to help them. And at best, they would end up with a baby. Either way, they would know within a few weeks. So Owen and Kira sent the facilitator her fee and the money for living expenses and they were officially matched with Darcy.

In the next few days Owen and Kira made arrangements to take leave from their jobs, researched flights and motels in the city where Darcy lived, and told their parents what was happening. They couldn't quite bring themselves to set up the nursery again, but the grandparents were ready to spring into action when the time came. Their hearts raced whenever the phone rang, and every few days Kira would check in with the facilitator, but after almost three weeks, Darcy still hadn't gone into labor. One day Kira asked the facilitator if she could check with Darcy to see if perhaps the due date had been miscalculated, and the facilitator confessed that Darcy hadn't been returning her calls for the past week. She added that she hadn't wanted to alarm them before knowing for sure that anything was wrong, but that this wasn't a good sign. There was another week of high anxiety before Owen and Kira settled into depression and the knowledge that they would never hear from Darcy again.

The facilitator was very sorry, and, true to her word, she was soon sending them information about other pregnant women. This time Owen and Kira opted not to be matched with anyone who had substance abuse or mental health problems. Their reasoning was not so much that they feared that the baby would be damaged or genetically predisposed to these problems but that they felt it would be too risky to place their own emotional well-being in the hands of someone they couldn't fully trust.

Owen and Kira waited another six months before they were matched with Janiva, who was thirty-seven and already had four children, between the ages of six and seventeen, with her husband. They had separated two years earlier, though never officially divorced, and Janiva had had a brief relationship with the man who was the father of this baby. He was married, more than willing to sign relinquishment papers, and extremely anxious that his wife not find out about his affair. Janiva and her husband were talking about a reconciliation, and neither of them felt prepared to raise this child. That all sounded good. The only negative was that the due date was six months off, which meant Owen and Kira would be spending a lot on living expenses. Six months plus the two months after delivery would amount to almost $9,000, money that was nonrefundable if Janiva changed her mind about adoption.

Owen and Kira talked with Janiva, with the facilitator on the line as well. They found it easy to talk with her, felt comfortable with the idea of ongoing contact after the adoption, and decided to go ahead despite the financial risk. Contact after that was primarily by text, so Owen and Kira didn't get to know Janiva the way they had gotten to know Lindy. That was unfortunate in a way but also a relief, since they couldn't allow themselves to fully emotionally invest in the situation. Kira also worried that if they spoke to Janiva, she would be able to tell that they were holding back. Their attorney was handling all legal and practical matters, and he told them everything was proceeding smoothly.

Owen and Kira waited for something to go wrong. But when both the baby's father and Janiva's husband (who also had legal rights to the baby) sent back their consents to the adoption, they allowed themselves to hope.

Then one amazing morning they received a call from Janiva telling them she was going to be induced that afternoon, two weeks early, and they should get there as soon as they could. Janiva's doctor was concerned about her blood pressure and had decided it was safer for everyone to deliver the baby early. Owen and Kira scrambled, still in a fog of caution and disbelief, and were on a plane five hours later. They got to the hospital shortly after the baby was born and were holding him that evening. They were also holding their breath.

Meeting Janiva was hugely reassuring, and when not only her husband but two of her older children came to the hospital to meet the baby and "his parents," Owen and Kira's hopes soared. The baby was a good weight, despite his early arrival, and was doing well enough to be released from the hospital on day two. Owen and Kira took him to a motel and waited for word from the attorney, who was scheduled to go to court the next afternoon. When he called to say that the parental rights had been terminated and they now had legal custody of the baby, Owen and Kira sobbed with relief. Then they called their stunned parents, who thought they had just gone on a brief vacation, and told their principals that substitute teachers would be needed.

Five days later they joyously brought the baby, whom they named Jack, home and settled in to being new parents. Kira's mother and some friends had come over and reassembled the nursery so everything was ready for a baby again. Owen and Kira had an additional week of parental leave together before he returned to work, while she planned to be home for another three months. They had managed to save quite a bit of money during their long wait for Jack, but the adoption had depleted those resources and more, so Kira was going to have to go back to work sooner than they had hoped. That wasn't so bad, though, because Kira's mom had taken one look at Jack and decided it was time for her to retire. She was more than willing to become his caretaker if Kira needed to work.

The adoption had taken a lot longer and cost a lot more than Owen and Kira had expected. It had been three years since they had signed up with the first attorney. Including the initial home study, attorney fees for Lindy, two years of online advertising fees, fees to the attorney in Florida, facilitation fees for Darcy and Janiva, living expenses for Darcy (one month) and Janiva (eight months), the fee to update their home study, the cost of airfare and a week in a hotel, fees for Janiva's attorney, the fee for the postplacement adoption report, and the attorney's fee to finalize the adoption, they had spent almost $60,000 and were deeply in debt. It was going to take a while to pay that off.

CHAPTER THREE

~

Why Is Adoption So Hard?

Why is adoption so hard? The simplest answer is that adoption is hard because there are so many more families wanting to adopt than there are babies who need to be adopted. Statistics about infant adoption are extremely difficult to pin down, in part because few formal records are kept on this type of adoption. Adoption professionals are likely to keep track of their own placement statistics, but there is no organized method for collecting information from them or from the adoption attorneys involved in private adoptions. Another complicating factor in understanding infant adoption statistics is that the more formal information on adoption, such as that available from the Census Bureau or general court records, doesn't distinguish between the various types of adoption. For example, there is no clarification with respect to the age of the adoptee at the time of placement, whether the child is being adopted by a nonrelative, or if the child was previously involved with the foster care system. The more accessible—and much more relevant—"statistic" currently available on Google suggests that there are approximately thirty-six families hoping to adopt each baby who becomes available for adoption. This is startling information (even to my jaded eyes), and while I'm not sure how this number was arrived at, it seems an accurate indication of how hard it is to adopt a baby these days.

The more complicated answer to the question about why adoption is so hard requires a look at the history of infant adoption. I'll use my own career trajectory to explain. In the early 1980s I began working as a counselor for a very large and well-respected adoption agency. Its efforts were primarily focused on international adoption, but the agency also had an innovative infant adoption program that promoted open adoption at a time when that was still quite unusual. The infant adoption program emphasized respectful and unbiased counseling for birth parents (at a time when that was definitely un-usual) and urged them to fully consider other possibilities, including parenting, when making their decision about adoption. This was during the Reagan administration, and conservatives eagerly embraced adoption as an alternative to abortion; consequently, the agency's infant adoption program received substantial funding through a federal government grant. In order to receive the grant, the agency had to agree that counselors would not discuss abortion with their clients, a stipulation that was awkward and misleading since the stated purpose of the infant adoption program was to help pregnant women fully explore *all* their options. The grant was a godsend, though, in that it allowed the agency to hire numerous counselors over a four-state area. At its peak, the agency's infant adoption program completed nearly one hundred adoptions a year and was instrumental in effecting change regarding openness between birth and adoptive parents. For a number of years, I acted as a supervisor to the birth parent counselors and consequently gained a broad overview of the issues they and their clients faced. I also acted as an adoption counselor, so I was equally aware of the issues from the perspective of the adoptive families I knew.

My belief, during the years I worked at that agency, was that their approach, with its emphasis on unbiased counseling and open adop-tion, was by far the most ethical approach to infant adoption. I was suspicious of private adoption, which didn't often provide for any sort of counseling—and certainly not unbiased counseling—for the birth parents. I was also suspicious of the religiously affiliated adoption agencies that promoted the belief that all babies belonged in two-parent, heterosexual households that shared the agency's religious views. Not only wasn't the counseling they provided unbiased, but birth mothers were often given the not-so-subtle message that relinquishing their babies would bring them God's approval—a stance that seemed especially coercive.

I worked quite happily for this agency for ten years, feeling good about the services we provided and the ethics of our approach. The infant program accounted for a relatively small number of our total adoptions, with the primary emphasis on international adoptions. In the 1980s, babies and young children from Korea (including my own youngest daughter) made up the greatest number of the agency's placements, and there were also children of all ages, many of them with special needs, coming from various other countries to be adopted by American parents. The agency funded numerous charitable efforts that helped provide safer, healthier, and more secure lives for the children in those countries who, for one reason or another, were being raised in orphanages. It was a privilege and a joy to be involved with that agency.

It was easy for the infant adoption program to thrive during the years in which it received federal funding. It was also easy for the agency to attract expectant women considering adoption during an era in which few other agencies offered any sort of openness or ongoing contact with the adoptive families. But things got more difficult when the grant ran out and at the same time other agencies began updating their attitudes toward openness. Even more significantly, adoptive parents began to embrace the idea that they could assert more control—especially financial control—over the adoption process by doing a private rather than an agency adoption. It gradually became harder for the agency I worked for to attract both birth and adoptive parents.

Periodically I would find myself wondering why, once the adoptive families and pregnant women the agency worked with had met each other, they didn't just decide to leave us behind and do an adoption on their own. What was stopping them? Not only could the family save a lot of money on agency fees, they and the birth parents could avoid the sometimes annoying policies and requirements of the agency.

This question came to a head for me after a mother who had no medical coverage experienced an especially difficult delivery and lengthy hospital stay, running up bills that the family she had chosen couldn't immediately pay. During the pregnancy, she hadn't wanted to apply for state provided medical assistance, even though she qualified, and the adoptive family had agreed to cover her medical bills, expecting a normal delivery. But the situation had changed and now the financial assistance was needed.

The agency needed to think about its bottom line, which included its ability to continue providing assistance to children in other countries who were in dire need. It couldn't justify absorbing an enormous medical bill, knowing full well how much good that money could do for so many other children. The contract the family had signed stipulated that all bills must be fully paid prior to placement of the baby, but they just didn't have the money. The director of the agency felt the solution was to ask the girl to choose a different family—one that was able to cover this expense. Needless to say, both the baby's mother and the adoptive family went berserk at this suggestion. Fortunately, after several days of turmoil and unhappiness, the hospital social worker stepped in and pointed out that the baby was still in his mother's custody. She was the one responsible for the medical bills and she qualified for state assistance. It turned out to be an easy process for the mother to apply for coverage retroactively, and the entire problem was solved before mother and baby were discharged from the hospital.

The larger question remained unanswered, though: What, exactly, had been preventing the mother from placing the baby with that family on her own? Couldn't she have told the agency she no longer required its services and arranged to do a private adoption? What "hold" did (or should) the agency really have over any of these people and the decisions they wanted to make about how to handle their adoption? If the large medical bill hadn't been covered by the state, would these particular birth and adoptive parents somehow have been obligated to give up their own wishes in order to financially benefit the agency and its good works? Would the agency have legal and/or ethical grounds to compel this mother not to place the baby with her chosen family? And was there a better way to approach infant adoption?

These questions eventually led me to join forces with a very small agency that acted as a hybrid between agency and private adoption, the crucial difference being that legal custody of babies went directly to adoptive parents rather than to the agency, as was traditional. This feature not only appealed to birth and adoptive parents but allowed the agency to dramatically reduce both its fees and its legal liability, which appealed to me. Over time, a partner and I became the agency's codirectors and renamed it Adoption Connections (no affiliation with any agencies of the same or similar name in other states). We were able to work with enough clients to keep the agency afloat, but not so many that we couldn't devote a great deal of time and attention to each of them.

We felt like we had found the sweet spot for adoption agencies. We operated on a small budget and worked primarily from home offices, so we could keep our fees low compared to larger agencies. The combination of low fees and lots of personal attention kept our adoptive parents happy, and we were free to provide whatever attention expectant parents considering adoption needed. Adoptive families also liked the fact that we charged a flat fee that committed us to working with them until they successfully adopted a baby, no matter how long it took and, consequently, how low our hourly rate got. If we'd paid more attention to the budget, we probably wouldn't have been so satisfied, but being able to do adoptions the way we felt they should be done was so rewarding that the money seemed secondary. We worked this way for about fifteen years, until the proliferation of adoption facilitation services and the practice of paying living expenses for expectant mothers prompted us to make a change.

One reason we could afford to keep the agency functioning despite its financial inefficiency was that my codirector and I also maintained private practices. I functioned—and still do—as a counselor specializing in all aspects of adoption, and I also write the various reports people need in order to complete an adoption. It is in this capacity that I know families who are adopting through other agencies, adoption facilitators, and attorneys.

In the early 2000s, I worked with a number of same-sex couples who adopted through adoption facilitation services, and I was delighted by the speed with which their babies arrived. I was not, however, delighted by the high total fees they were paying and by the fact that they usually didn't have any sort of ongoing contact with their children's birth parents. These were families I had counseled during the home study about the benefits of open relationships, and they had seemed to embrace the concept, so I wondered why it had been decided against in the end. I discovered that most of the families had paid living expenses for the expectant mothers, many of whom were dealing with significant hardships, including substance abuse, domestic violence, criminal records, and mental health concerns. Many of these women also had other children they were not raising. Sometimes the women had voluntarily placed their children with birth relatives or with adoptive parents; other times the women had involuntarily lost custody to the child's other parent or another relative or to the state. All these women seemed to need far more help, financial and otherwise, than the pregnant women with whom I usually worked.

Adoptive parents have always been expected to pay for what are termed "adoption-related expenses." These typically include any agency or facilitation fees, legal fees, medical fees, counseling fees, maternity clothing, transportation expenses to medical appointments, and miscellaneous pregnancy-related expenses. All states have laws against giving or receiving money in exchange for a baby, but they have very different ways of interpreting those laws. In Washington, where my agency is licensed, it is necessary to get court approval in order to provide financial assistance to expectant parents considering adoption. Of course, there is no law against people giving money to other people, but adoptive parents in Washington who give money to expectant parents without court approval leave themselves vulnerable to charges of coercion. A birth mother who wanted to undo an adoption could claim that she did not really want to relinquish her parental rights but felt financially pressured to do so, a charge that might be viewed sympathetically by a judge.

When I worked for the large agency, attention to financial scruples was extreme. Counselors often met with pregnant women at a neutral (not our office, not their home) location of their choice, and this was often a restaurant. But the rules were so strict that we could offer to pay only for drinks, not a meal. It was assumed that payment of anything over a few dollars could be construed as coercive. Things were more relaxed at my own small agency, and our ads specified that "all allowable adoption expenses" (medical, legal, counseling, maternity clothes) would be covered, but everything else required court approval. Few women asked for any sort of financial assistance beyond what was routinely approved, but occasionally an emergency arose and we could get approval for the adoptive family to pay for an electric bill or a phone bill in order to keep those services from being discontinued. It was even possible to ask for approval to pay for a month or two of rent, as long as the payment went straight to the landlord. Those requests were rare, although I did get one call in the early 1990s from a woman who responded to my "Hello" with "I heard I can get $5,000 for my baby. Is that true?" I explained about the need for court approval in Washington, and she hung up.

In the early days of Adoption Connections, most of our clients found their babies through newspaper advertising, with a typical ad drawing sufficient attention to make our average wait time for a baby a surprising nine months. Starting in about 2010, most of the families we worked with switched to online advertising and posted their profiles on adoption websites to attract prospective birth mothers. This widespread advertising seemed clearly beneficial for birth parents, since they would have a far wider choice of families, and for adoptive families, since their profiles would be viewed by a far greater number of potential birth mothers. Neither of them would be limited by geographical parameters or by the scope of whatever adoption professional they were using. But a quickly apparent downside to this widespread advertising, for the adoptive parents, was that they were suddenly competing with hundreds (and soon, thousands) of other families. More than ever, they needed a way to stand out from the crowd, and it didn't take long for people to figure out that the most effective way to do that was by offering money.

Once adoptive parents started competing with one another for the attention of expectant mothers on a national and sometimes even international scale, scruples about financial coercion began to disappear. It soon became commonplace for the families I knew who were using the services of adoption facilitators to pay monthly living expenses for the women they had been matched with, sometimes for as long as six or seven months. It wasn't long before many agencies adopted the practice as well, having little choice but to go along with this change in attitude toward the ethics of financial compensation. After all, pregnant women couldn't be expected to reject the readily available offers of financial assistance and the usually perfectly great families who were making those offers in favor of agencies that were sticking to an (apparently outdated) ethical stance. It felt to me as though we went from complete rejection to complete acceptance of the practice of routinely paying living expenses before anyone really stopped to consider what was happening or how it would change the adoption process.

One of the undesirable changes was a dramatic increase in the cost of adoption, which seemed to almost double in the space of a few years. The cost of infant adoption has always varied widely and therefore been extremely difficult to estimate with any accuracy. However, statistics from 1999 indicate that the average infant adoption cost somewhere between $8,000 and $30,000; by 2020 that average had risen to between $35,000 and $45,000. It is important to remember that these figures reflect only the cost of a successful adoption. Families may also spend substantial amounts of money pursuing scams or other situations that do not result in the placement of a child. I know many families who have lost between $5,000 and $20,000 in this way, making the average amount of money families spend in their effort to find a child somewhere between $35,000 and $60,000. And there are certainly families whose total expenses are far higher than these averages.

Another undesirable change was an almost immediate increase in the number of scam calls from women falsely claiming to be considering adoption. Scams had certainly existed before, but they had been mercifully rare for the families I knew. Usually, once it was obvious that no money was going to be forthcoming without an attorney's involvement, a scammer would give up and go away. She may have wasted our time and emotion, but little or no money would have been lost. Offering to pay monthly living expenses seemed like an open invitation to scammers, and for the first time I began hearing from families who had lost many thousands of dollars paying for the living expenses of women whose babies were not ultimately adopted by that family or anyone else. It's impossible to know whether these women had a change of heart after the birth of their babies, whether they had never felt really comfortable with the idea of adoption but had been keeping their options open, or whether they had been scamming from the start.

Having come from a social services background, my codirector and I felt uneasy about this more business-oriented approach that had taken over much of adoption. We were concerned about the ethics of attracting pregnant women through large ad campaigns promising financial support but providing little in the way of counseling, let alone unbiased and professional counseling. Although we could see that this new method was effective in finding babies for adoptive families, we felt uncomfortable being part of it. Something fundamental had changed.

I went through an anxious period during which I often envisioned myself in a courtroom trying to explain what exactly our agency had done to warrant our up-front flat fee. I wondered how I could convince people that our counseling was always unbiased even though we got a big payoff (in the form of being able to stop working for that particular family) when women relinquished their babies. I imagined myself telling the judge about the expert quality of our services and all the hours we had devoted to counseling for many months before and after the adoption, helping the pregnant woman find the medical care and other services she needed, helping her choose what she felt was the perfect adoptive family for her child, helping both the birth and adoptive families negotiate their relationship with each other and plan for ongoing contact, and continuing to provide counseling and support to both the birth and adoptive parents and to the child far into the future, for as long as they felt they needed us—not to mention being available 24/7 pretty much whenever anyone wanted to talk. I knew that our agency provided an abundance of time and care to our clients, but I also knew that our financial structure looked a lot like those of adoption professionals who did not provide this type of service.

So we got out of the baby-finding business and I stopped having worrisome visions about having to defend adoption finances. In fact, it eventually become evident to me that my worrying was completely unnecessary because adoption agencies and facilitators who embraced the business model have rarely been asked to defend themselves. Instead, they have been operating successful businesses and placing lots of babies in adoptive homes, often quite speedily. But I don't regret the decision we made. We just couldn't be comfortable operating in a way that allowed for what felt to us like ethical compromise, no matter how adversely this decision affected the agency's bottom line.

Beginning in the early 2000s, many of the same-sex couples I worked with found their babies thorough adoption facilitators. I was happy for them, but when I later visited their homes to do the postplacement report, I found that the parents rarely spoke enthusiastically about their experience with the facilitator. They also rarely developed ongoing relationships with their child's birth parents, even though that had almost become the norm for adoptive families. These parents would talk freely with me about their unhappiness with the facilitator, but they did not take steps to make any sort of formal complaint, even when they felt that they and/or their child's birth mother had been treated unethically.

The first time I seriously questioned what was happening with a facilitator was sometime around 2005, when a gay couple I worked with was matched with a woman who identified herself as a prostitute and was in jail for drug-related offenses. She didn't know who the father was or what race the baby would be. The couple had paid the facilitator's fee and was expecting to pay legal fees and any uncovered medical expenses. Several months before the baby was due, the woman was unexpectedly released from jail. Suddenly the family was confronted with the need to not only pay her living expenses but somehow convince her not to resume her drug use or life on the streets. Through amazing effort and expense, they succeeded at both these things and also at adopting a wonderful baby girl. When that child was about six months old, the facilitator called them to say that their baby's birth mother was pregnant again and wondered if they would be interested in adopting her next baby. Once again they paid for all of her living expenses, along with the facilitator's fee, the legal fees, and any uncovered medical expenses. This time they adopted a baby boy. When their children were not quite two years old and not quite one year old, the facilitator called again, and the men made the painful decision not to adopt their children's half sibling.

I was delighted for them when these men brought home their first baby. I was also delighted when they brought home the second baby, even though I was concerned about another unplanned pregnancy for this woman. But after the third pregnancy I was no longer delighted about anything. I was instead certain that these pregnancies had been financially motivated and that the facilitator not only knew this but was "facilitating" these pregnancies for her own financial gain. The whole situation seemed so egregious I couldn't believe it was legal. I was very naive.

CHAPTER FOUR

∼

Lindy

A Birth Mother's Story

Ethical changes in adoption practice haven't just affected adoptive parents; they have also changed the landscape for birth mothers. Owen and Kira's first adoption heartbreak does not begin to account for the story of Lindy, the birth mother of the child they lost to her father and his parents.

When Lindy was four months old, her seventeen-year-old mother hit the road with her boyfriend, leaving Lindy behind. She called home a couple times over the next few years and then effectively disappeared. Lindy's father was not the boyfriend but someone her mother had sex with at a party. Nothing more was known about him, and he presumably was unaware of Lindy's existence.

Lindy was a shy and sensitive child, raised by her grandmother in a quiet home that suited them both. But their well-ordered lives came to an end when Lindy was seven years old and her grandmother got sick. Lindy's aunt moved into the house after the grandmother's first surgery, bringing along her two teenage sons. The aunt, who worked full time, was a single parent and her grandmother's caretaker. She had no extra time to devote to Lindy, and the boys mostly ignored their little cousin. Although the house no longer felt so safe and quiet, Lindy was content just to be with her grandmother. When she wasn't at school, she spent most of her time curled up on the bed or in a nearby chair, reading or watching a silent television while her grandmother slept. It wasn't until her grandmother died, when Lindy was ten, that everything went so terribly wrong.

Lindy was bereft without her grandmother and expressed her grief by withdrawing emotionally and rejecting any overtures of comfort. But on nights when she was just too lonely, Lindy sometimes sought comfort by crawling into bed with her fifteen-year-old cousin. When he started molesting her, Lindy felt frightened, confused, and more lonely than ever. She also felt that if her aunt found out what was happening she would blame Lindy, and that's exactly what eventually did happen. At age eleven, after a concerned teacher referred Lindy to the school counselor, the story of the abuse came out. The aunt reacted defensively, refusing to believe that her son could behave that way and labeling Lindy the aggressor. Further counseling with the aunt revealed her deep anger at the suffering Lindy's mother had caused the family and her ongoing resentment about the hardship of having to raise her sister's daughter. It was decided that Lindy should not continue living with her aunt, and since there were no other relatives available, she was sent to her first foster home.

As children often do, Lindy believed she was to blame and that being sent away was a punishment she must have deserved. Her first foster mother was kind, and Lindy began to warm up to her and never directly caused any trouble. Even so, the placement didn't last long. Lindy's quiet and cooperative nature seemed to elicit jealousy and cruelty in another child, and since that girl had been in the home much longer, Lindy was the one who had to go. Her caseworker tried to soften the blow by explaining to Lindy that it would be easier to find a new home for her than for the other girl. It didn't make things easier for Lindy, and she got the clear message that her own needs would not be prioritized.

The second foster home was with an older couple, and Lindy appreciated the quiet routine and lack of drama in her life with them. She was able to focus on school, worked hard to please her teachers, and was relieved to find that academics was an area in which she could excel. Although she was too cautious to make any close friendships, Lindy was not victimized at school, and she even took part in a few of the youth activities at the church her foster parents attended. Things went well for Lindy for three years, until her foster father had a heart attack and died. Her foster mother sold the house and moved to another state to live with relatives, leaving Lindy to find a new home.

The third foster home was what Lindy's caseworker called a "teen home" and it functioned like a group home rather than a family home. At almost fifteen, Lindy was the youngest, with four other girls between the ages of fifteen and eighteen. The foster parents were an outgoing couple in their forties who had both worked in actual group homes and were considered experts in dealing with teenagers. The girls in the house all had "issues," including problems with substance abuse, minor criminal offenses, and histories of physical abuse and sexual abuse. Lindy's own history of sexual abuse apparently suggested to her caseworker that she would fit in well with them. But although Lindy was only slightly younger than the other girls physically, she was socially and emotionally many years younger. She had developed few of the social skills needed to nurture even normal peer relationships, so Lindy was totally unequipped to handle the complicated dynamics these girls presented. As usual, Lindy kept a low profile and didn't cause difficulty for anyone, but she was frightened and overwhelmed by the older girls. She made every effort to avoid interacting with them, hoping to avoid conflict, and was amazed when one of the seventeen-year-olds decided to take Lindy under her wing. This girl, Maia, became the first close friend Lindy had had since grade school, in a relationship in which Maia dominated and Lindy was content to follow her lead.

Maia left the foster home as soon as she was eighteen and moved into a house with her boyfriend and some other people. Lindy visited on occasion and was flattered by the attention of one of the guys who hung around, a twenty-year-old named Matt. Her foster parents were concerned about a possible relationship and tried to talk to her about birth control, but Lindy insisted that she wasn't interested in Matt and had no intention of having sex with anyone until she was much older. While it may not have been her intention to have sex, Lindy did become pregnant a month before her sixteenth birthday and was stunned by this turn of events. She was in such denial that she couldn't acknowledge the possibility of pregnancy, even to herself, until well into the sixth month. It was obvious to everyone, especially Lindy, that she wasn't ready to be a parent, so she agreed to go with her foster mother to meet with an attorney who handled adoptions.

Lindy approached the task of planning an adoption in the somewhat dazed and unassuming manner with which she had approached the rest of her life, and her general passivity made it hard for anyone to figure out what she really wanted. Her foster mother, her caseworker, and even the attorney all tried to get her to talk about her feelings and whether she was really sure about doing an adoption. They told her that giving up the baby would probably be the hardest thing she would ever do in her whole life. Lindy assumed they knew what they were talking about and that giving up a baby would be hard for most people, but that things were going to be different for her. She had never really been around babies, didn't find them particularly appealing, and definitely didn't want to be a mother yet, if ever. She felt detached from the baby and also from her own feelings. Nothing new about that.

But when the day came to start looking at adoptive family profiles, Lindy suddenly came alive. As soon as she saw the book that a couple named Owen and Kira had put together, Lindy began to focus on them and the life they could give her baby. They had written such a good letter, all about how much they loved each other and their families and how much they wanted to be parents. They sounded so nice, and best of all, they were both teachers. Although she had always been far too shy to acknowledge it, Lindy had been very much affected by the interest and kindness shown by several of her teachers. Maybe Owen and Kira would be like that.

After meeting them, Lindy liked Owen and Kira even more, and they seemed to really like her too. They were interested in everything about her and always wanted to know how she was feeling, not just physically but emotionally. Owen and Kira were even considerate toward her when Matt, whom Lindy had identified as the father, told the attorney that he didn't want to sign anything and that there were plenty of other guys who could be the father. Owen and Kira told Lindy they believed her when she said it wasn't true.

Despite her young age and lack of knowledge about her body, Lindy didn't find the pregnancy too difficult. She was tall, carried the extra weight relatively easily, and generally felt good physically. She also felt pretty good emotionally, and in some ways she was happier than she had been since her grandmother's death. Lindy suddenly found herself the recipient of what felt like genuine care and attention. The baby still seemed completely unreal to her, and she never second-guessed her decision to plan an adoption. Each time she met with Owen and Kira it strengthened her belief that adoption would be right for all of them.

Lindy gave birth to a beautiful, healthy baby girl, with Owen and Kira at the hospital for the delivery. The three of them were together in Lindy's room the following day, admiring the baby, when the attorney arrived. His appearance wasn't unexpected, but what he had to say certainly was. Kira crumpled to the floor with a cry as the attorney explained that the father's mother had contacted him and was insisting on paternity testing. If the baby was her son's, there would be no adoption. Lindy was mute in response and just turned to the wall, unable even to look at anyone else in the room. Over the next few days paternity was established, the grandparents were given temporary custody of the baby, and Lindy withdrew into silence.

It turned out that Maia was the one who had contacted the grandmother. She had objected to the idea of adoption all along and couldn't understand how Lindy could "just give away" her baby. Maia knew Matt had moved out of state without telling his parents about the baby, and she didn't think that was right either. So she had taken matters into her own hands. It turned out that the grandmother shared Maia's disdain for women who could give away their babies. It also turned out that the grandmother and her husband were only in their mid-forties, were perfectly capable of raising another child, and wanted to be given the chance to raise their granddaughter. Maia believed Lindy would thank her someday.

Lindy returned to the foster home. In a few days Owen and Kira sent her a nice message, asking how she was doing and if they could visit. Lindy could only think about how painful a visit would be for all of them. She had wanted to make them happy and instead had hurt them so badly. What could she possibly say to them now? What good could come of seeing each other again?

The court ordered her to have visitation with the baby, but Lindy was so unresponsive at the visits that they were soon discontinued. Lindy was put on antidepressants and saw a counselor, with no discernible improvement. It was eventually decided that Lindy might be a suicide risk, and she was sent to an inpatient treatment program for several weeks, then to a therapeutic group home, where she lived for the next three months before returning to her foster home.

Her counselor at the therapeutic group home was able to focus some of their sessions on plans for the baby's future, and Lindy made the decision to relinquish her parental rights and allow Matt's parents to adopt their granddaughter. She decided that they must really love her since they had fought to keep her, and Lindy didn't see that she really had another choice. She just hoped Matt's parents would never tell the child that she had been unwanted or that her mother had tried to give her away. Lindy's own feelings about the baby stayed well beneath the surface and she continued to feel stunned by all that had happened, as though she had been swept along by an icy tide that left her numb.

Lindy was able to meet the requirements for high school graduation by taking online classes and earned her degree before she turned eighteen, with no plans to attend college, no ideas about what she wanted to do with her life, and no one to guide her. She had three different caseworkers during her years in foster care, and the latest one had been on the job only a few months. Lindy could have continued living in the foster home and gotten help with school or some type of job training, but she had never developed a bond with the foster parents, and there were now a couple of girls living in the home who made life difficult for her there. The caseworker was able to help her find a job at a restaurant where she could earn enough to afford a room in a house, and Lindy really liked the thought of having a room all to herself. She especially liked the idea of not being a foster child anymore. So shortly after her eighteenth birthday, Lindy left the house where she had lived for three years without forming any real attachments to anyone there. Her counselor maintained contact for a while, but for all practical purposes Lindy was on her own.

Social life was a little easier for Lindy now that she was on medication. She was able to interact successfully with some of the other people in the house, and when she started drinking with them, her social life suddenly blossomed. Alcohol paved the way to what Lindy considered friendship and romance, and she soon became an eager participant in socializing with her roommates. Not surprisingly, Lindy enjoyed drinking, since it helped her to relax and enjoy herself and to forget about the hard times she had endured. It wasn't long before drinking became an almost nightly habit. There were lots of guys around, and Lindy was in and out of "relationships" with several of them, just like the other girls in the house.

When Lindy discovered she was pregnant again, she immediately thought of Owen and Kira and how sad they had been after losing the first baby. She worried they might be mad at her, but Lindy found the courage to contact the attorney and was genuinely happy for them when he told her that Owen and Kira and just adopted a baby boy. The attorney urged Lindy to come in and look at profiles for some of the other adoptive families he represented, and as before, Lindy never really allowed herself to consider an alternative other than adoption. She felt quite sure that she didn't have whatever qualities it took to be someone's mother.

This time Lindy met with several families before making her decision. They were all really nice to her and it was hard to choose, but she finally decided to go with John and Becca. John was a dermatologist and Becca worked in his office but planned to stay at home once they had a baby. Becca was the sort of person who liked to take charge of things, and she sort of reminded Lindy of Maia, but in a really good way. She was interested in every single aspect of Lindy's pregnancy and wanted to go to all her doctor's appointments, always asking the doctor a bunch of questions that Lindy hadn't thought to ask. Becca also liked to take Lindy out to lunch and shopping for maternity and baby clothes. They even got pedicures and massages together. Her attention made Lindy feel cared for.

One day when Becca came early to pick Lindy up for an appointment, she had to wait for a bit and couldn't help but notice signs of last night's party at the house, including a very hungover guest asleep on the couch. In addition to a lot of bottles, there was evidence of drug use and there appeared to have been some sort of altercation resulting in overturned furniture. Becca was extremely concerned and wasted no time in persuading Lindy to move. Becca said she and John would be more than happy to pay for an apartment in order to make sure that Lindy was living in a safe place. They had also discussed it and decided that they preferred that Lindy not continue working at the restaurant and wanted to cover all her expenses from then until two months after the baby was born. Lindy was stunned and impressed. As with the first pregnancy, she felt physically good and quite capable of continuing to work, but she wasn't going to turn down John and Becca's generosity, especially since she figured they probably knew better than she did what was best. So Lindy moved to an apartment by herself and relied almost entirely on Becca for any sort of social interaction. The two of them often took long walks together and got to know each other pretty well. Lindy didn't share a lot with Becca, though, and quite naturally she mostly listened while Becca did the talking. When Lindy did say something, it was often in an effort to reassure Becca that she would not change her mind about the adoption.

Everything went smoothly during the delivery. The baby was another beautiful little girl, whom they named Maisie, and John and Becca barely put her down during the entire two-day hospital stay. Lindy saw this as evidence of what good parents they were going to be and only held Maisie once, handing her back quickly when she thought she saw an anxious look on Becca's face. The father had signed the consent forms ahead of time, so the attorney was able to go to court even before Maisie was released from the hospital.

John and Becca said goodbye to Lindy when they all left the hospital together that afternoon. They had arranged for Becca's mother to take Lindy back to the apartment, and the new grandmother, who was an older version of Becca, was effusive in her praise of Maisie and of Lindy's generosity and sacrifice. She helped Lindy into the apartment, then spruced things up by arranging the vases of flowers that friends and relatives of theirs had sent to the hospital and surprising Lindy with several grocery bags full of fancy prepared foods. She even plumped the pillows and made a cozy place for Lindy on the couch, covering her legs with the gift of an amazingly soft new blanket. Most surprising of all, the grandmother's eyes filled with tears as she kissed Lindy goodbye and wished her well. Not since her own grandmother's death had Lindy experienced this sort of tenderness. But then the new grandmother left.

The following weeks were lonely. Becca and John were good about staying in touch, and they did just what they said they would by texting lots of pictures of Maisie, but Lindy didn't know out how to react. She didn't even know how she felt. She was amazed by Maisie's beauty and was proud, though a bit disbelieving, that she had created someone so perfect. She did not regret her decision and took pleasure in thinking about how happy her baby's life would be, but happiness in her own life seemed unattainable. John and Becca were concerned about Lindy and convinced her to see the grief counselor that the attorney recommended. But the sessions with the counselor barely scratched at the surface of Lindy's unhappiness. She decided that she preferred to try ignoring it altogether.

Two months after Maisie's birth, Lindy got a job in another restaurant. She couldn't afford the apartment on her own, so when John and Becca stopped paying her rent, Lindy moved into a house with some people she knew from her new job. John and Becca still sent pictures, and they paid for counseling until Lindy told them she didn't think she needed it anymore. By the time Maisie was five months old, Lindy was well settled in her new house with a new set of roommates—and a renewed habit of getting drunk with them. From outward appearances, Lindy's lifestyle seemed fairly typical of a young person who liked to party, hadn't figured out what she wanted to do in life, and wasn't ready to settle down yet anyway. She was only twenty-one and it seemed like she was having fun, like the others, except Lindy had fun only when she was drinking. She was still conscientious about her work, she was still a considerate housemate, and she was still generous and undemanding in her relationships, but Lindy was emotionally removed from everything unless she was drinking.

Lindy thought she had figured out birth control after her second pregnancy, so the third one really caught her off guard—at least that's what she told herself. This time the father was a man she had been seeing for a while, and when she told him she was pregnant he said he wanted her to keep the baby and that he would take care of them both. Lindy believed him for a couple of months but wasn't too surprised when he broke up with her, saying he just wasn't ready for a child. Neither was she, she decided.

Lindy had figured out some other things in the past few years as well. One of them was that people had been really good to her when she was pregnant and planning an adoption. The other was that she really missed being treated like that. It wasn't that she specifically missed Becca or Kira or even the babies; what Lindy missed was the kindness they had offered. She understood that it was conditional kindness and that none of them would have bothered with her except for the babies. Even with the baby, John and Becca were no longer really a part of her life. But Lindy had powerful memories of the care and respect they had all shown her, even the counselors and the attorney had been kind, and it made sense to her to try to relive those times.

Lindy knew that John and Becca hoped to adopt another baby, ideally when Maisie was three, but she assumed they'd be okay with an almost two-and-a-half-year difference in ages and would want to adopt this baby too. Instead of being happy when she told them she was pregnant though, John and Becca were terribly upset. It turned out that they had gone ahead with the adoption of a baby boy just two months earlier, even though Maisie was only nineteen months old. The new baby was fussy and Maisie was having a hard time adjusting; although they struggled with the decision for several weeks, John and Becca very sadly concluded they just wouldn't be able to handle having three children under the age of two and a half.

The third time was not a charm for Lindy. The attorney told her he was concerned about her lifestyle and the amount of drinking she had done during the first trimester, before acknowledging to herself that she was pregnant. He explained that he would have to disclose that fact to any prospective adoptive families because people would be worried that her drinking might have affected the baby. Since she hadn't been trying to get pregnant, Lindy hadn't thought that her drinking was a problem at the time, but now she felt frightened and guilty. It seemed that she always messed things up, even when she thought she was just acting like everyone else. The girls in the house all drank and had sex with different guys, and as far as Lindy knew, none of them had ever gotten pregnant. She didn't understand why she always seemed to do things wrong.

Lindy was able to find another nice adoptive family, though, and as with the second pregnancy, the attorney arranged for them to pay all her living expenses if she would agree to move into an apartment by herself and promise not to use any alcohol or drugs. This wasn't a hard promise, since Lindy had never used drugs and was now terrified by what she had been told about using alcohol during pregnancy, but she was hurt and embarrassed by the suggestion that she might deliberately continue to endanger the baby. It was hard for her to feel close to the family after that, and they didn't make any overtures to get to know her better. This was so different from the way both Kira and Becca had acted that Lindy decided the new couple must dislike her, and she felt she could understand their attitude. But when she managed to ask the attorney if something was wrong, he assured her that the new people just felt shy and anxious because they wanted a child so much. Lindy was relieved and found it endearing that they felt shy and anxious—feelings with which she could easily identify. When the baby was born, a boy this time, he was smaller than the girls had been and seemed sort of fragile, but he was in perfect health and the couple was ecstatic and effusive in their adoration and appreciation. It made Lindy feel good to see them so happy, and she was enormously relieved that there was nothing wrong with the baby.

Two months later, when Lindy's period of free rent at the apartment was over, there was a room available in her old house. She moved back in, got her job back at the restaurant, and thought she would resume her old lifestyle. The family told her they would pay for her to see a counselor for six months, and this time Lindy made good use of the offer. Instead of focusing on Lindy's troubled history, this counselor helped her focus on what she called "practical matters," such as what she wanted to do be doing with her life. Lindy had no idea what that might be, but she liked the idea of going back to school to try to figure it out. She signed up for a math class at the community college, finding the work easy even though she had some catching up to do since she had completed only the minimum requirements for high school graduation. The next semester she took biology, found it fascinating, and especially liked the quiet time she spent working in the lab. The social life going on at her house was distracting, and Lindy spent as little time there as possible, preferring to study in the library. At the end of the semester, when she got an A in biology, Lindy was ecstatic and allowed herself to dream about the possibility of someday becoming a nurse.

The problem was that she could only afford to take one class each semester, and at that rate it would take her ages just to complete her associate's degree. Lindy knew that other people got financial aid in order to pay for college, and though it terrified her to be in debt, she decided it would be worth it in the end, so she took out a loan. She was then able to take almost a full load of classes and complete her degree in two years. Lindy worked full time while she was in school and wasn't able to devote as much time to studying as she wished she could, but she still maintained a high B average. One of her professors encouraged her to go on for a bachelor's degree, but Lindy was eager to get out in the work world and pay off her loan before incurring any more debt.

She was also eager to get a better job so that she could finally move out of the house and away from the party lifestyle that everyone else who lived there still enjoyed. It had been so hard to study there. But after a six-month search, Lindy hadn't been able to find a job that paid any better than waitressing.

Lindy worked at the restaurant for another year and barely made a dent in repaying her loan before finally accepting the fact that this wasn't a workable approach. She needed to make more money, and the only way to do that was to go back to school—and the only way to go back to school was to take out another loan. A loan would pay her school expenses, but what about everything else she had to pay for? Even with a loan, Lindy was going to have a hard time financially. Somehow she needed to reduce her living expenses, but she was already living as cheaply as she possible could. Lindy thought back to the days when she was pregnant and lived in the apartments by herself. She'd felt lonely at the time, but those apartments would have been the perfect place to study. It would be so much faster and easier to get through school if she lived someplace like that again.

The attorney was surprised when Lindy called to talk about another adoption, and he was shocked when she told him that she wasn't pregnant—yet.

CHAPTER FIVE

~

Where Does All the Money Go?

For the first half of my career, it was rare for the pregnant women I knew to ask for any additional financial assistance beyond an allowance for maternity clothing. This was true for women working with traditional adoption agencies as well as for women working directly with attorneys on private adoptions. Legal, medical, and counseling fees specific to the adoption were routinely paid for by the adoptive family, and in an emergency situation, an adoptive family could seek court approval to help out with unexpected expenses; for example, if a woman planning an adoption had been supporting herself by working in a job that became difficult for her in later pregnancy, the hopeful adoptive family could get court approval to provide some months of rent or pay for utilities or some similarly specific expense. But every financial transaction was carefully monitored, and any deviance could be seen as coercive and possibly even grounds for overturning an adoption if the mother later claimed she had been financially pressured to relinquish her parental rights. These regulations were put in place to prevent financial coercion of both the birth and adoptive parents, and they seemed to work fairly well in that respect.

That situation changed with the emergence of adoption facilitation services (as distinct from licensed adoption agencies) and the acceptance of a more business-oriented (as distinct from social service–oriented) approach to adoption. For facilitators, the focus was on wide-scale advertising and making the maximum number of "matches" between pregnant women and prospective adoptive parents. Legal matters were handled as they would be for a private adoption, with custody of babies going directly to the adoptive parents rather than to an agency, an approach that pleased both birth and adoptive parents. The most significant and distinct advantage, or lure, that facilitators offered pregnant women was to connect them to adoptive parents who would pay their living expenses throughout the pregnancy, a practice traditional agencies found unacceptable. I cannot tell you why this was not seen as coercive, but for whatever reason, the practice of paying living expenses was largely unregulated and wildly successful; adoption facilitators were able to attract the attention of pregnant women, adoptive families working with facilitators were able to adopt more quickly, pregnant women were getting financial support, facilitators were making money. What's not to like?

From my perspective as a counselor, a great deal. It took some years for the change to take place, but traditional agencies eventually realized they'd better revise their thinking about the ethics of adoption finances if they wanted to stay in business. Pregnant women revised their feelings about the ethics of accepting money, and adoptive families revised their feelings about the ethics of giving money. There was a general feeling of "everybody's doing it" that mitigated the sense of unease surrounding these financial arrangements. It suddenly seemed easy for everyone involved to feel comfortable with financial transactions that had previously been all but forbidden.

Of course, adoptive parents weren't happy about the increased expense, and a number of them had to give up as the cost of infant adoption skyrocketed. There wasn't a lot of sympathy or incentive to improve things for the remaining families, who were often erroneously viewed as wealthy people who could well afford to pay for something as precious as a baby. In truth, these hopeful adoptive parents were usually part of average middle-class families. They had simply come to the conclusion that they were willing to do whatever they had to do to bring a baby into their lives, even if that meant going deeply into debt.

Adoption agency fees had already been high, but they were generally set fees. This allowed families to plan accordingly and to continue working with the agency at no additional cost until they succeeded in adopting a baby. In contrast, families working with adoption facilitators paid a lower fee up front but were also expected to cover any case-specific charges, which often could not be predicted. If, for example, a legal situation turned out to be more complicated than expected, the adoptive family would need to pay that actual legal fee, rather than paying a traditional agency's set fee for legal expenses. It was also true that if for any reason an adoption being handled by a facilitator didn't go through, the adoptive family would typically lose a portion of the money they had spent. If they chose to continue working with the facilitator, they could apply the fee, or a portion of it, to the next possible adoption, but they would once again need to pay for legal and living expenses for the new birth mother—and just hope that the next adoption went through. It was possible to lose a whole lot of money this way and still not have a baby.

You might well ask why families wanted to work with adoption facilitators if the financial risks were higher than they would be with an agency. The answer is that facilitators were attracting pregnant women who were considering adoption away from traditional adoption agencies by offering to pay their living expenses. Consequently, the wait time for a baby was generally shorter, often significantly so, for people who worked with facilitators. Adoptive families and adoption agencies that didn't offer to pay for living expenses had a hard time attracting the attention of pregnant women, without whom there are no babies to adopt. This is how the exchange of money began to change and control not only the logistics but the ethics of adoption.

Considering how expensive adoption is, it would seem logical to assume that adoption professionals are well paid and work from well-appointed offices. This may be the case for some high-priced adoption attorneys or unethical adoption facilitators who manage to collect fees while providing little in the way of service, but it does not apply to the vast majority of adoption professionals. My first job in adoption, at a large and well-respected agency, barely paid the minimum wage. Despite my master's degree and seven years' experience, I was happy to accept this significant decrease in income, fortunate not to be the only breadwinner in my family, and content to work for lower pay if it allowed me to do work that I loved. Like me, most adoption professionals find the job rewarding for psychological rather than financial reasons. We are not getting rich, and we never expected that we would. So where is all that money going?

I believe the experiences of the families I know can serve to answer that question. The majority of their money was spent in the following ways, which I'll address separately, although there is necessarily a great deal of overlap.

Agency Fees: Adoption agency fees are high primarily because adoption agencies are, by nature, financially inefficient operations that provide services to a lot of people who do not pay for them. It's probably safe to estimate that a typical agency works with more nonpaying clients (pregnant women and their partners) than paying clients (the adoptive parents). This is because agencies provide counseling and other services to many women who do not ultimately choose adoption for their babies. Some women make this decision early in their pregnancies, prior to being connected with an adoptive family, but others do not decide against adoption until after the birth of the baby.

Like government-funded child welfare agencies, adoption agencies provide social services, but they do so without any taxpayer support. Traditionally, non-state-run adoption agencies were nonprofit entities, often funded by churches or other organizations that provided a significant percentage of their budget. Agencies without this sort of affiliation usually operated on a shoestring, and those that have been able to stay in business probably still do, despite their high fees. No one is really at fault; adoption agencies just have a bad business model, financially speaking. They may have high fees, but they also have high expenses and most have no source of funding other than adoptive parent fees.

Facilitation Fees: Unlike governmental organizations and traditional adoption agencies that provide social services, most adoption facilitation services function with the very specific goal of connecting pregnant women and adoptive parents as efficiently and inexpensively as possible. Facilitators might have counseling credentials (though this is not a requirement) and hearts of gold, but their mandate is usually simply to help people connect. The facilitator then typically passes the situation on to an attorney or agency to finish the job and complete the adoption. The reason people who work with facilitators might lose money is that too often the job does not actually get finished. I don't know what sorts of statistics facilitators keep about their success rates, but I do know many families who have paid facilitation fees for connections that fell through. I suspect that many facilitators advertise their match rates rather than their completed adoption rates (similar to an IVF clinic advertising the number of clients who achieve a pregnancy rather than the number who deliver a baby).

Attorney Fees: Attorneys are paid by the hour, and although that hourly rate is usually high, families used to be able to fairly reliably predict what they would have to pay in total legal fees for an infant adoption. There were exceptions, of course, such as when a situation turned out to be unexpectedly complicated by something like the last-minute discovery of a second possible father or the disclosure of Native American heritage and the need to get approval from the tribe prior to an adoption. Families always knew about the possibility of legal fees being higher than predicted, but most of them (and their attorneys) didn't have to deal with these expensive complications. That no longer seems to be the case.

These days, attorneys are being asked to handle enormously complicated legal situations, often involving birth and adoptive parents who live in different states with different legal requirements. Attorneys are likely to be involved earlier in the process, before the expectant mother—who is asking for support—has made a solid decision about adoption. They are also more likely to be providing legal services in scams and other situations that don't end in an adoption. All this wasted money and expertise is not the fault of the attorneys, who are simply responding to the need created by the premature and irresponsible matching of pregnant women and adoptive parents that characterizes much of adoption practice today. The unfortunate truth is that we now have many situations that very much require the expensive advice of attorneys—often multiple attorneys—every step of the way. It didn't used to be like this.

Scams: Adoption scams break people's hearts, spirits, and bank accounts. There have always been scammers in adoption, and they have often been very hard to detect, but they have never been as prevalent or done as much damage as they do these days. Of course, that shouldn't be surprising, since we essentially lay out the welcome mat for scammers with ads that offer to pay living expenses for women "considering adoption." It's reasonable to assume that some women who are struggling financially and wondering how they will provide for the baby they are expecting might be tempted to "consider adoption" due to a come-on like that. And even though it is not reasonable, it is unfortunately true that there are also people in the world (some of them actually pregnant and some not) who are eager to take advantage of that offer with no intention at all of considering adoption.

Living Expenses: Families today must confront the reality that most pregnant women considering adoption today expect to have their living expenses paid for during the pregnancy and for several months after the birth of the baby. The total amount of money a family pays for living expenses varies widely, depending primarily on the stage of the pregnancy when the connection is made and the cost of living in the area where the woman lives. The bill is also subject to increases for unanticipated expenses, making it difficult for families to know what will ultimately be expected of them financially. Adoptive families who have agreed to pay living expenses will lose their "investment" if the woman ultimately changes her mind about adoption. If that happens, the adoptive family is faced with the likelihood of being asked to support the next woman whose baby they hope to adopt, once again with no assurance that they will actually end up adopting that baby. Obviously, this can get very expensive.

Perhaps I know an exceptionally unlucky group of people, but I would estimate that the majority of the families I have worked with in recent years have had to contend with a combination of the factors listed above that contribute to high adoption fees. They have paid facilitation fees and/or attorney fees and/or living expenses for adoptions that didn't go through, and they have lost time and money on scams. Many have been blindsided by unexpected expenses, sometimes opting to go into debt and sometimes needing to back away from that particular adoption. The families who opted to work with traditional agencies (and paid high agency fees) fared better with respect to unexpected legal expenses, but they still risked losing whatever they spent on living expenses if an adoption fell through.

One of our society's widely believed truisms is "You get what you pay for." We also generally believe that the more worthwhile or valuable something is, the more expensive it is likely to be. Whether we're searching for a pair of shoes or the services of a brain surgeon, our assumption is often that the more we have to pay for what we want, the more likely we are to be happy with our purchase. We may be unhappy about the expense, but we feel we will ultimately be rewarded by having purchased a superior item or service. Obviously this idea doesn't hold true when we are talking about the price of an infant adoption. Babies aren't products. It is absurd to think that some are more valuable than others, and there is zero correlation between the love adoptive parents feel for their children and the amount of money they have spent on their adoption. One can, however, assign a value to the quality of service adoptive parents receive during their adoption process.

In the past it may have been true that higher fees for an infant adoption reflected a higher level of service provided to both birth and adoptive parents, but that is no longer the case. In fact, high adoption fees these days seem more likely to be related to especially complicated and risky situations than to the quality of service anyone is receiving. And unlike in most businesses, if an adoption agency appears to be too financially successful (fancy office, slick advertising, etc.), both birth and adoptive parents might wonder how wisely and ethically their money is being spent. Adoption professionals sometimes walk a fine line between appearing to be motivated solely by the altruistic desire to create happy families and appearing to be making money off the misfortune of others.

CHAPTER SIX

~

Yes, It's Legal

I periodically get email that reads something like this:

Are you working with any families currently who would be interested in these situations?

1. Melissa and Ron
Birth parents: Caucasian
Due date: 3/3
Health: Physically healthy. Birth mother has depression, diagnosed bipolar, learning disability and ADHD. Birth father has ADHD and learning disability. Denies drug or alcohol use.
Birth mother has five children, not parenting any of them.
Asking for $900 a month living expenses. Total cost estimate at $35,000.

2. Briana (father unknown)
Birth parents: Caucasian
Due date: 9/26
Health: Diagnosed with depression and anxiety, on medication. Denies drug or alcohol use.
Has three children living with other family members.
Asking for $1,000 a month living expenses. Total cost estimate at $38,000.

3. Teresa
   Birth mother: Caucasian and African American
   Birth father: African American (whereabouts unknown)
   Due date: 8/20 Boy
   Health: Has been diagnosed with bipolar, ADHD, schizophrenia, but
   not taking any meds. Denies drug or alcohol use; smokes.
   No other children.
   Asking for $1,600 monthly living expenses. Total cost estimate at
   $42,000.

These messages are from adoption agencies or facilitators who are contacting me (and no doubt many other adoption professionals) because none of their regular clients is interested in adopting these babies. These are all what are called "high-risk" situations, and it is supposedly hard to find families for the babies. But the truth is that there are lots of families who want very much to adopt them, even though these babies are at increased risk for ongoing difficulties. The thing that can be a bit difficult is finding families able and willing to pay the birth mother's living expenses and the fee the agency/facilitator is charging to connect them with her. A high price has been attached to these babies, and it severely limits their options in life.

The way this system generally works is that the pregnant woman contacts the agency/facilitator in response to an ad promising that living expenses will be paid to women considering adoption for their babies. Let's say the woman is in the third month of pregnancy, is struggling financially to care for several other children, and has come to the conclusion that she just doesn't have the ability to provide for another baby. She contacts the agency/facilitator and talks to someone who is understanding and reassuring, offering both financial and emotional assistance. The two speak about what the woman is hoping to find in an adoptive family and what she needs in the way of financial support during the pregnancy. These two people are unlikely to live in the same geographical area, so they don't meet in person and most likely never will.

If there is nothing discouraging about the woman's situation—such as substance abuse or mental health concerns—she will be told about various families working with that agency/facilitator. Hopefully she will find what she feels is the perfect family for her baby and everything will progress smoothly. But in a high-risk situation, the agency/facilitator might need to broaden his or her search. This is the point at which he or she will begin to reach out to other adoption professionals, hoping that one of them will have a family that this woman will "choose." The search is no longer for the perfect family but simply for a reasonably appropriate family. The woman's choices, and her baby's options, have narrowed considerably. Of course, the pregnant woman is free to decide to look elsewhere at this point, but she is struggling financially and knows that the monthly support payments will start only after she chooses a family. So the pressure is on.

Meanwhile, a waiting adoptive family has just been contacted about this situation, sometimes directly by an agency/facilitator who has seen their online profile and sometimes by an adoption professional who has passed along this "connection" from the agency/facilitator. The family has probably been given very limited information and is being asked to make a decision, usually within a day or two, about whether or not they are interested in working with this woman. In many cases families are asked to financially commit to the adoption without ever having spoken to the pregnant woman. In other cases they are allowed to speak with her but only with a financially interested third party on the line to monitor the call. At this point everyone is feeling pressured. The pregnant woman wants to start receiving living expenses, the agency/facilitator wants to receive the fee so she can stay in business, and the adoptive parents are being asked to write a large check and sign up with an agency/facilitator they've only just heard of in the past few days.

Once an adoptive family is "matched" with a pregnant woman, the family is typically asked to pay approximately half of the agency/facilitation fee and to start paying the woman's monthly living expenses. The other half of the fee is payable prior to the placement of the baby. In the event that the adoption does not take place, for any reason, the adoptive family can often either request a refund of half the fee they have already paid or continue to work with the agency/facilitator. As is the case with private adoption, money that has been spent on living expenses and legal fees for this particular situation are nonrefundable. If the family does continue to work with the agency/facilitator, they will be expected to pay legal and living expenses for the next prospective birth mother—money they will once again lose if that adoption doesn't go through. Although it is certainly troubling that an adoptive family stands to lose so much money if the pregnant woman changes her mind about adoption, there is nothing unusual about this situation or these expenses. Financial arrangements like this are now the norm. It is also common for adoption facilitators to set a time limit on their services, and families who have not been successful in adopting a child within that time will often be required to pay additional fees if they wish to continue working with the facilitator.

There are several things about these high-risk situations that are particularly concerning. First, the agency/facilitator is highly motivated to connect the pregnant woman with a family as quickly as possible, thereby ensuring (as much as it is feasible to do so) that she will continue to work with this agency/facilitator. The speed with which these matches are made brings into question the degree of care that is being taken to collect and verify information about both the pregnant woman and the adoptive parents. Second, adoptive families are asked to make what will surely be one of the most important decisions of their lives in great haste and with little information. I acknowledge that sometimes adoption decisions do need to be made quickly and with insufficient information, but I strenuously object to the idea that this should happen largely because one or more of the parties involved are eager to get the money flowing. Third, both parties to this agreement are denied the opportunity to get acquainted prior to making a commitment to each other. I understand that the pressure in these situations often comes from pregnant women who are desperate to start receiving financial assistance, but we must figure out a different way to relieve that financial pressure. Receiving needed financial assistance should not be dependent upon entering into a hastily made agreement to relinquish one's baby.

As the director of an adoption agency, I am well aware of the need to pay attention to the agency's bottom line, and I am not accusing other adoption professionals of knowingly being financially coercive or cold-hearted in their approach to any of their clients. I am, however, pointing out that certain financial realities inherent in this type of adoption actually encourage coercive and coldhearted policies and behavior. The argument that pregnant women have greater financial need than they did in the past, when paying for living expenses was rare, simply strengthens the case that we are not doing enough as a society (rather than as individual adoptive parents) to meet their needs. And the idea that adoptive parents, as distinct from all citizens, should feel financially responsible for alleviating the financial needs of pregnant women willfully ignores what then becomes the transactional nature of these arrangements.

It seems safe to assume that most adoptive parents are kind people with good intentions, and they certainly care about the well-being of the women who give birth to the children they hope to adopt, but kindness is not what prompts them to pay for living expenses. These payments are primarily a reaction to the laws of supply and demand and the desire to be successful in an extremely competitive marketplace.

Paying for living expenses for expectant mothers has become commonplace in at least the past two decades, and as far as I have observed, this practice hasn't corresponded to any increase in goodwill between birth and adoptive parents. In fact, I would say the opposite is true. It's my impression that there has instead been an increase in wariness on the part of adoptive parents. This wariness is a logical response to an increase in the number of scams as well as in the number of planned adoptions that fall through after the payment of a significant amount of money in living expenses. Adoptive parents are obviously going to be unhappy about losing large sums of money in these situations, and their connections with other expectant mothers can be influenced by these negative past experiences.

It isn't only adoptive parents who feel uneasy about these financial arrangements. I also believe that pregnant women would feel far more comfortable receiving assistance in a more formalized, less personal manner—one that didn't require them to make pleas/requests/demands to individuals and that didn't tie the assistance they need to the relinquishment of their baby.

It is especially revealing to see how the attitudes of pregnant women and adoptive parents toward these financial arrangements have changed over time. Early in my career, the idea that women would ever be offered money for their babies was widely viewed as abhorrent, probably even more so by the women than by adoptive parents. These women were already struggling with widespread misunderstanding of their motives for relinquishing, along with their own feelings of sadness and guilt about not feeling able to raise their baby. While they certainly knew how much they loved their unborn child and that they were planning an adoption because they wanted their child to have a life they felt unable to provide, they also knew that most people didn't understand their true motivation. These women were aware that many people cannot imagine any circumstance in which they would voluntarily relinquish their parental rights, and as a result, they often felt misunderstood, vilified, and vulnerable to condemnation.

For most of the twentieth century, pregnant women and adoptive parents were kept far apart by the people who handled adoptive placements, on the assumption that this approach was in everyone's best interest. This adherence to anonymity was supposedly put in place to spare women the shame of their pregnancy, to spare adoptive parents the shame of infertility, and to spare children the shame of being labeled "illegitimate." The 1970s and 1980s brought significant social change—namely, the ready availability of birth control, the legalization of abortion, and an increased acceptance of single parenthood—which resulted in a steep decline in the number of babies available for adoption. For the first time, there were far more people wanting to adopt infants than there were babies needing adoptive homes. This created a situation in which pregnant women could exert some control over the adoption process, and the first things they requested were to be able to choose their babies' adoptive parents and to have some form of ongoing contact and reassurance that the child was thriving. These parents made it clear that the enforced secrecy and shame surrounding adoption was a reflection of outdated societal values, did not reflect their wishes, and had never served them well. Their sentiments were echoed by adoptees who also felt angry and misrepresented by adoption professionals who had accepted the idea that shame and secrecy were an inherent part of the adoption experience. Even adoptive parents were able to embrace the concept and practice of open adoption once they realized how damaging the old system had been.

Attitudes toward birth parents changed dramatically, as did attitudes toward adoption overall, when open adoption became common. As birth and adoptive parents got to know one another, their fears diminished and empathy grew. Everyone benefited—most of all the children who were now being raised without the secrets and stigma that had previously colored adoption.

Adoption is a lifelong undertaking and should not be viewed as a one-time event in which a family acquires a baby and then proceeds to ignore the child's heritage. It is true that in the past, adoptive parents were urged to forget all about where the child had come from and "raise them as if they were your own" (giving clear voice to the misguided idea that children who were adopted aren't, in fact, our real children). But those days are gone, and even if we hadn't come to the conclusion that secrecy in adoption was harmful to everyone involved, the easy availability of genetic testing has made it impossible to sustain that secrecy. Adoptive families today must also recognize the fact that long before they have access to genetic testing, many children have a facility with social media that makes it easy to connect with people online with even the smallest bits of information. Secrecy in adoption is no longer a realistic option.

The benefits of openness for all members of the adoption triad are well established and have been accepted practice for at least the past few decades. With the caveat that openness is not appropriate in every situation, my conversations with adoptive parents about ongoing contact with birth parents are typically skewed in favor of openness. This means not that birth and adoptive families will, or necessarily should, have a great deal of contact with one another, but that they are familiar and comfortable with each other and could pursue contact if they chose to do so. There is no expectation of secrecy and there is an acceptance of the idea that the person who has been adopted, rather than either the birth or adoptive parents, will be the ultimate decision maker with respect to future contact.

CHAPTER SEVEN

~

Middlemen

The middlemen in adoption are the people hired by prospective adoptive parents to help them pursue their dream of a having a baby. These middlemen might include attorneys, adoption facilitators, adoption counselors, adoption consultants, and full-service child-placing agencies. They also might include people and services used only for specific purposes, such as a website to place ads attracting pregnant women or a "boutique service provider" who helps create an appealing family profile. The services of all these middlemen come at a price, of course, and they range in value from priceless to worthless.

The vast majority of people who choose to work in adoption do so with good intentions. Many of them have a personal connection to adoption and fully understand how complex the subject is and how important it is that they do their jobs well. Unfortunately, there are also people acting as adoption professionals who have good intentions but insufficient skills; worse, there are some genuinely unscrupulous individuals motivated by what they see as an opportunity for financial exploitation. Discrepancies in the expertise of service providers, as well as in the overall quality of the service they provide, are found in most businesses, but given the nature of adoption, it is especially painful, not only financially but emotionally, when things go wrong. It is also especially tempting, when things have gone wrong in an adoption, to blame the middlemen—and in some cases that blame is well deserved.

It used to be true that there were two basic ways to adopt an infant in this country: With some exceptions, people chose between private adoption and agency adoption. People choosing private adoption would need to select an attorney and people choosing agency adoption would need to select an agency. Once that was accomplished, the attorney or agency would guide them through the process. Either way, adoption was a relatively straightforward undertaking compared to what people go through today. One important difference was that most people chose to work with attorneys and agencies that were in their geographical area. While there usually weren't a large number of options available to them, people were able to actually meet with the professionals they were considering before making a decision about which one to trust with such an important undertaking.

Decisions about who to work with were also made easier by the fact that the reputations of agencies and attorneys were built on their history of service, and there was usually a consensus about who did or didn't do a good job. It was most likely true that if a family worked with a reputable agency or attorney, they could expect to have a reasonably good experience and outcome. Although adoption was still likely to be a stressful and unpredictable process, families generally had confidence in the attorney or agency they had chosen, and this confidence helped them get through difficult times without losing faith that they would ultimately be successful in adopting a baby.

Compare that to the multiplicity of options available to people who want to adopt an infant today, and to the likely geographical distance and infrequency of contact between families and their middlemen. It is not surprising that the increased distance, both physically and psychologically, between adoptive families and their middlemen would lead to increased discontent.

The internet has made things both better and worse for adoptive parents. Things are better in that hopeful adoptive parents have access to a far greater number of professionals and others offering their services, but things are worse in that it has become extremely difficult to assess the quality of service that all these people are providing. A Google search on "infant adoption" produces what at first appears to be lot of options, including agencies, facilitators, and attorneys specializing in adoption. Most of them have lovely pictures of babies and their happy adoptive parents. That feels encouraging until further research reveals very little in the way of information about who actually does a good job or how to go about finding this information. There is no approved rating system for adoption providers, although there may be opinions in reviews or adoption chat rooms. But even in these informal settings, positive reviews about a particular person or service often seem more like an organized effort to drum up business than an objective assessment, and very negative reviews can seem like personal (and maybe unrealistic) reactions to disappointment rather than fair and useful evaluations of the service provided.

Adoption is such an emotionally fraught undertaking that people can't be expected to be objective about it, so customer satisfaction is likely to be a reflection simply of whether a family achieved their goal of adopting a baby. Unfortunately, achieving that goal might have nothing at all to do with how skilled or attentive or ethical the middlemen were. In fact, truly unethical middlemen, who have no qualms about financially coercing women to relinquish their babies or otherwise skirting accepted standards of practice, are probably the ones who can boast about having the quickest adoptive placements. As a result, these people may well have highly satisfied clients who are quite content not to question the ethics behind the ease of their adoptions and want only to focus on being happy new parents. It's hard to blame them for that. And an agency that has provided many months of ethical and unbiased counseling may be the focus of a family's anger and disappointment (and a bad review) when a woman simply decides against adoption for her baby in the end. The family's unhappy response may be unfair, but it is understandable.

Families are generally reluctant to say anything negative about the middlemen who connected them with their baby, but once that baby is safely in their custody, some of these now-happy people do want to talk about the negative experiences they have been through. I become aware of their stories when I visit with families to do the postplacement report, but it is only well after the adoption has been finalized that many people feel they can talk freely. Even then, they are anxious not to be seen as whistleblowers and are rarely willing to make any sort of formal complaint, even anonymously, about truly egregious abuses.

The most frequent complaint about middlemen I hear from adoptive parents is that they felt unsupported and/or they felt the birth parents were unsupported by the people they had paid to guide them through the adoption process. The adoptive families were often geographically distant from both the middlemen and the expectant mothers, and there was no opportunity for in-person contact between them. Families complained that information provided about the expectant parents was extremely limited and that they were expected to commit financially to the middlemen, and emotionally to the whole situation, within just a few days of first hearing about it. Often people were required to send money before being allowed to speak with an expectant mother or, if they were allowed to speak to her, the middleman had to be present on the call as well. Once the money had been sent and the match had been made, adoptive families complained that services came to a halt. Phone calls to the middlemen were not returned in a timely manner and it was extremely difficult to get information. They felt there was no one available to act as an advocate or counselor for either themselves or the pregnant women. Sometimes middlemen had made it clear from the start that their job ended once the match was made, but more often they were vague on that subject and families felt abandoned at a crucial time.

Waiting adoptive parents are loath to do anything that might jeopardize an adoption, and most would wait throughout the pregnancy—if not patiently, at least without complaining enough to risk alienating their middlemen. When things went wrong and a particular placement fell through, the adoptive parents usually opted to continue working with the middlemen because they had already invested considerable money that would be lost if they went elsewhere. This was true even for adoptive parents who felt the middlemen had been seriously negligent.

Families sometimes expressed unhappiness about what they felt had been a lack of support during the birth and the hospital stay. They told me about their distress after they had been summoned to the hospital, hoping to be present for the delivery, only to discover that no one there was aware of or prepared for what was supposed to be a planned adoption. Instead of receiving assistance and reassurance from the hospital staff, the adoptive parents found themselves the targets of suspicion and subject to rules that prevented their access to the baby.

These misunderstandings were usually fairly short-lived, but the damage was done. Hopeful adoptive parents who arrive at the hospital full of the joyous anticipation of momentarily meeting their baby and instead face hours of helpless and unnecessary delay have endured a sad introduction to adoptive parenthood that is not easily forgotten.

Even worse are the too-common instances in which adoptive parents are viewed warily by the hospital staff. I've heard more than a few stories from families who were made to feel like baby snatchers by nurses who had experienced unethical adoption practices in the past and were now doing their best to protect their patients from similar mistreatment. This scenario can usually be avoided if the middleman communicates with the hospital social worker to let everyone know that this particular adoption is being handled properly. But often there is no such communication (and sometimes there is no such adherence to proper handling), and adoptive parents must negotiate their interactions with the hospital staff on their own.

Another common complaint with interstate adoptions (and many infant adoptions are interstate in these days of internet matching) involves the waiting period before a family is allowed to take a baby home. A new adoptive family needs to obtain permission to transport a baby from one state to another, and the process typically takes anywhere from three to ten days. Families must put up with the inherent uncertainties of government bureaucracy, but they should not have to endure delays caused by their middlemen. It is unacceptable, for example, to ask a family to spend extra time waiting to bring their baby home simply because the person at their small agency or facilitation service who typically handles the task of applying for interstate approval is unavailable, as happened to a family from Washington who had traveled to Florida for their baby. They hadn't realized just how small the agency they were working with was until they were told they would have to stay in Florida until the woman who knew how to complete the necessary paperwork for an interstate adoption returned from vacation. I think small operations often provide the best service, but adoption is a business that requires irregular hours and emergency coverage, and an essential service should not be dependent upon only one person's knowledge or availability.

Families sometimes involve me in their decision-making prior to contracting with middlemen. Typically they have found the middle-man through online advertising that sounds very appealing, primarily because it is advertising significantly quicker and cheaper adoptions.

Several years ago I worked with a couple who felt sure they had discovered the perfect agency. They told me the agency had placed one hundred babies the previous year and that total fees were capped at $20,000. I expressed skepticism and explained that if those statistics were true, the adoption world would be abuzz with the news and everyone would be rushing to that agency. The family agreed to check further and came back with the news that they had somehow misunderstood; the agency had actually placed twenty babies the previous year, and while the agency fee was never more than $20,000, there were other expenses such as attorney fees, birth mother living expenses, advertising, and so on that "could" run the price up a bit. In other words, it was probably going to be just as expensive as any other agency. Deliberately or not, this agency representative chose to explain the financial reality of their adoptions in a way that was misleading. The family decided to use the agency anyway and wasted about a year and a lot of money before unhappily parting ways.

A relatively new type of middleman is the "adoption consultant." Once again, the value of this type of service varies widely. I am normally skeptical about the need for extra middlemen, but there are exceptions. Several years ago I did a home study for a couple who were very excited about working with a middleman—actually a middle-woman—who provided consultation/advocacy services for adoptive parents. She was an adoptive mother who felt she had gained a level of expertise during her own adoption process that would be of benefit to others. At the time, this woman charged $2,500 (now $3,600) and promised to be available for support and information, to keep all the family's paperwork organized, and to use her connections to seek out babies for her families to adopt. She also referred families to another middleman who, for an additional fee, would help them create their profile. My initial reaction, again, was skepticism. It didn't seem that this woman was offering much that I wasn't already doing as a family's home study provider. I'd always kept their paperwork in order, I typically helped people create their profiles (good ones!), and I was usually available for consultation free of charge. I didn't seek out babies for them to adopt, but I did let waiting families know whenever I heard about a possible connection for them. I wondered what it could be that this woman was actually going to do for her clients. I had a slightly tense, clarifying conversation with her and then waited to have my suspicions confirmed.

Instead, a baby girl arrived two months later, and I was delighted to be proven wrong. Another family I had done a home study for also decided to work with this woman. The placement took six months this time, which is still considerably quicker than average, and a baby girl joined that family as well. So how does this woman do it, and why aren't other people having the same sort of success?

Obviously a sample of two isn't statistically significant, but I expect that the experiences these families had are fairly typical of what one can expect when working with this particular middle-woman. Her website says that her clients typically wait only a few months for a baby and that she will charge no unexpected fees. In the case of the two families I worked with, their babies came through the consultant's connections with what she called "partner agencies," whose fees they were expected to pay. This raised some questions:

1. Why was the average waiting time quicker for families working with the consultant than it was for families working directly with the partner agencies but without the consultant's assistance?
2. Why were the agencies looking outside of their normal pool of clients for families for these particular babies?
3. Were total expenses for the families working with this woman lower than total expenses for families working directly with the partner agencies?

It appeared to me that families working with this consultant had been able to zoom to the top of the waiting list, and while I was very happy for them, it seemed there must be more to the story.

There was. In both cases, the birth mothers of the babies my families adopted had histories of drug use throughout their pregnancies. One of the women tested positive for hepatitis C and had suffered from postpartum depression since the birth of another baby just fourteen months earlier. One of the birth fathers was a heavy meth user and the other was listed as "unknown," making the termination of his parental rights more complicated and risky. It seems likely that the consultant's families were able to adopt so quickly because the agency's regular clients were unwilling to take on the possible problems these situations presented. It is evident that the consultant's services are benefiting her partner agencies by finding them families for pregnant women their regular clients avoid. It also seems evident that this consultant is doing a good job of advocating for her families, who are getting babies quickly, and that they feel they are getting their money's worth from her.

It's easy to see that being "partners" works well financially for the consultant and the agency, but not so easy to understand how the adoptive parents are benefiting by working with, and paying, both of them. Instead, the extra fees for the consultant seem to have "bought" them the opportunity to take on extra risk and pay a higher fee than they would have if they'd worked directly with the agency.

In some ways these arrangements remind me of the relatively recent real estate trend that has convinced sellers they need to "stage" their homes in order to be competitive. This helps the realtor (who finds it easier to sell staged homes), but either the buyer or seller is going to end up paying for the staging. It isn't cost-free; nor is paying for an extra middleman cost-free for an adoptive family.

Why did we suddenly decide that homeowners need to spend thousands of dollars to stage their homes in order to sell them for top dollar when people always used to sell homes for top dollar without the extra expense? Why have we decided that adoptive families need to spend thousands of dollars on additional middlemen when they used to work directly with an agency or attorney without the extra expense? I think the answer is a seemingly contradictory combination of "because everyone else is doing it" and "because it will give me an advantage" over other families. Adoptive parents don't trust the old system to work well enough on its own and feel they need the help of these extra middlemen. Just as realtors don't want the houses they are trying to sell to be among the few that are unstaged, adoptive parents don't want to compete in this highly competitive market with an "unstaged" profile, ad campaign, and the like.

Despite my objections on principle to the need for extra middlemen, I will happily work with any who make the adoption process easier for families. The particular middle-woman who worked with my two families recently impressed me by deciding that she would no longer work with one of her partner agencies because they had made one too many mistakes, and she no longer felt comfortable recommending them to families. In this adoption marketplace it is almost unheard of to cut ties with a potential source of babies, so her willingness to do so is ethically impressive. At the same time, both of the families who used this middle-woman had concerns about the experience and opted not to work with her again.

For what it's worth (which is essentially nothing), an internet search reveals six reviews and a rating of 3.7 stars for the agency the middle-woman is refusing to work with any longer. There are three five-star ratings from families who successfully adopted babies and two one-star ratings from the same unhappy person who gave the agency money but still doesn't have a baby.

~

CHAPTER EIGHT

Julia

A Single Adoptive Mother's Story

Julia is an impressive person. She is also an executive at a large company, is Black, and is the mother of two daughters who are nine and three years old. Julia married a man named Martin when she was twenty-three, shortly after completing her master's degree in business administration, and planned to devote herself entirely to her career until she was thirty and then start having children. She had always wanted a large family but felt she could adapt to the possibility that three was the maximum number of children Martin was going to feel happy about. Julia and Martin both worked long hours on weekdays, and there wasn't a lot of overlap in their recreational interests, so they didn't spend much time together on weekends either. For the most part, they seemed busy and happy, they rarely had any significant disagreements, and they both focused on their careers and on the shared goal of buying a house. Julia was happy thinking about the children they would raise in that home. Martin was happy thinking about it as a good investment.

In retrospect, Julia can easily see that she was as responsible for the ultimate demise of the marriage as her husband was, although he was the first one to acknowledge how far apart they had grown. This happened when Julia was thirty and announced that the time had come for them to have a baby. She had spent the past seven years assuming that she and Martin were in agreement about this, but his shock at the idea forced her to realize otherwise. When they finally took the time to really talk things over, Julia was further shocked to hear that Martin wasn't sure he wanted to have children at all. She had to admit that this wasn't the first time he had expressed the sentiment; it was just the first time she hadn't dismissed his feelings as absurd. Julia also had to admit that the idea of losing Martin was far less upsetting to her than the knowledge that doing so meant that she was going to have to postpone motherhood.

Julia is an extremely determined, competent, and action-oriented person who felt there was no time to lose in her quest for a child. She and Martin divorced promptly, and Julia spent the next four years dating a number of mostly very nice men, none of whom rose to the level of prospective father for her future children. Julia also continued to advance in her career and was able to buy a house on her own. But while she loved the house and loved living in a neighborhood full of families, being there intensified her own sadness at not having children. The empty bedrooms needed to be filled.

So, characteristically, Julia took action. She carefully researched various options for adoption and decided that the quickest way to get a baby into her home was to work through the state and become licensed as a foster-to-adopt home. She underwent extensive training in the process of getting licensed and felt truly distressed by much of what she learned about the foster care system. Her eyes and heart were opened wide by the stories of abuse and dysfunction that most of the children who come to the attention of child protective services have endured. But instead of being discouraged, Julia's determination grew stronger. Now she not only wanted a child, she wanted to offer love and stability to a child in need. She knew the risks inherent in a foster-to-adopt placement and felt strong enough to deal with them if it became necessary.

Julia began preparing for a baby shortly after starting the licensing process. She took baby care classes, read piles of books, and turned one of her extra bedrooms into a beautiful and well-stocked nursery. Not long after she was officially licensed, a caseworker contacted Julia about a baby girl named Morgan. Morgan had been born drug affected and weighing only four pounds, eight ounces. She had been taken into custody by CPS at birth due to opiate withdrawal and was described as tremulous and hypertonic. During her first month of life, Morgan had frequent bouts of projectile vomiting, could not tolerate bottle feeding, and needed to be tube fed. She was now two months old, weighed almost eight pounds, and had been taking a bottle for the past two weeks. She was doing well, all things considered, and would be ready for discharge as soon as an appropriate foster home could be found for her. The caseworker explained that there were still uncertainties with regard to Morgan's health and possible developmental issues, but what she needed most right now was to be in a home where she could form attachments. Julia said yes before she even asked about the situation with the birth parents and the likelihood that Morgan would ultimately become available for adoption. She could not wait to get that baby in her arms and help her "attach," no matter what might happen in the long term. The knowledge that Morgan had been parentless and alone for so many weeks was painful to think about, and Julia was committed to doing everything she possibly could to make up for that lost time.

Julia arranged to take four months of parental leave and enlisted the help of her mother and one of her sisters, both of whom were eager to be involved in caring for Morgan. All this support was invaluable to Julia and the days were quite manageable, but she was on her own at night, and after a week of sleeplessness, she found herself wondering how well she would be able to handle single parenthood after all. Morgan was an extremely fussy baby, and Julia's image of bonding with her as they gazed peacefully into each other's eyes vanished, replaced by the reality of countless hours of pacing the floor while Morgan screamed inconsolably in her arms. Respite came whenever Morgan finally fell asleep and bonding came in amazing rushes when she slept in Julia's arms.

The caseworker had told Julia that Morgan suffered from gastroesophageal reflux, various food allergies, and what were termed "sensory integration issues," believed to be related to prenatal drug exposure. She was also frequently congested, with breathing so loud it kept Julia awake at night, not because of the noise but because it terrified her to hear Morgan struggling to breathe. It took Julia about four months and numerous trips to the doctor to gain sufficient control over Morgan's symptoms to keep her (and Julia) adequately comfortable and happy.

Taking care of Morgan was physically and emotionally exhausting, but as soon as Julia got her bearings, her confidence returned and she tackled every challenge determined to succeed. Julia became an expert on reflux and allergies, and, whether due to Julia's efforts or to Morgan simply outgrowing the worst of her symptoms, by the time she was a year old, they had largely disappeared. Concerns about sensory integration also became a nonissue as Morgan got older. She was developmentally within normal limits at her one-year well-baby checkup and has consistently been in at least the top 20 percent on all measurements of intellectual achievement from the time she started preschool at two years old through the present. Morgan is now a confident, affectionate, energetic, and socially adept little girl.

Julia knows how very fortunate she was to have succeeded in adopting the first baby who was placed in her home, but she did not feel confident that that process would work out well for her a second time. Morgan's birth mother left the hospital only a few hours after delivering her baby and never returned to visit. The caseworker was unable to contact her or to obtain any information at all about Morgan's birth father. Nevertheless, despite feeling primarily optimistic, even the smallest degree of uncertainty was excruciating for Julia, and it took almost two years before she was able to finalize Morgan's adoption. I won't distress you with the details of all the setbacks (change of caseworkers, three months of parental leave for one caseworker, many months spent seeking extended birth family members, time wasted on inaccurate information about the putative father, etc.), but for Julia, they amounted to a lot of anguish. She very much wanted to adopt another child but did not want to put herself through the ordeal of a foster-to-adopt placement again.

Almost five years ago, when Julia contacted me about her desire to adopt a second child, I thought she would have an easy time. Her history of success with her first child, along with her willingness to adopt another child with similar special needs, put her in what I assumed was a much-sought-after category of adoptive parents. She was asking for a child of either sex, up to the age of five (Morgan's age at the time), of full or part Black heritage. Most significantly, she was willing to consider a child with a wide range of physical, developmental, and/or emotional challenges and had proven herself to be a wonderful advocate for just such a child.

My first question to Julia was, "Why aren't you working with the state?" The foster care system had an abundance of children, and one of them would have been placed with her in short order. But Julia explained that she had found the uncertainty of the foster-to-adopt program agonizing and felt it would be unfair for her to ask Morgan to endure something similar. I certainly understood her feelings about this but regretted that a child in the foster care system would be denied a mother like Julia. It also seemed regrettable that Julia was probably going to have to spend a lot of money on a private adoption, but she felt it would be money well spent if it protected Morgan from growing to love a little brother or sister who might ultimately be taken away from their family.

I expected that it wouldn't take long at all to find the right child to join Julia's family. I called people I knew at other agencies and raved about her, and everyone agreed that she sounded wonderful. They said they would keep her in mind if an appropriate situation came up, but apparently, and despite periodic reminders from me, it never did. Many months went by, and as I got to know Julia, I discovered that she was tireless (actually more like relentless) in her pursuit of a child to adopt. She was extremely thorough in her research and followed up on every possible lead, asking me to follow up if a social worker was required to make the initial contact with whatever entity had control over a child's future. I soon lost count of the number of inquiries she and I made. None of them resulted in anything promising. Often they didn't even result in a response.

Julia's first connection was with an adoption facilitator in another state who wanted to "present" her to a pregnant woman, but only after receiving a nonrefundable $8,000 and an agreement to pay $1,200 a month in living expenses, also nonrefundable. Julia asked to speak with the woman first and was told that wouldn't be possible until they had been "matched" and that a match couldn't be made until the facilitator had her money. Julia concluded that she couldn't take such an expensive gamble on this situation. She needed to have some sense of who the pregnant woman was and why she was making the decision to relinquish her child, and the tidbits of information the facilitator provided were not reassuring.

Julia told me that she had set a $35,000 adoption budget and had given herself a one-year deadline to find a child. If she was not successful within those parameters, she would give up and decide that it just wasn't meant to be. As time passed, the parameters changed and Julia found herself pushing out the timeline and agreeing to take risks she never dreamed she would have to take. A number of "matches" ultimately fell through, but finally, two and a half years and about $55,000 later, Julia brought home Andrea, the baby girl who fulfilled her dream for a second child. She found her through the services of an adoption law center.

I'm going to start little Andrea's story by telling you that she is now a joyful, beautiful, bright, and healthy toddler who is developing normally in all respects and is a constant source of delight to her mother and big sister. But life did not start out well for her. At birth, Andrea was limp, had a very low heart rate, and was not breathing. She was put on a CPAP, which provided mechanical ventilation, and was assigned an APGAR score of 1. After a week in neonatal intensive care, Andrea was able to breathe on her own but struggled with feeding and reflux. Her weight decreased for a while, but miraculously, at three weeks she started doing well enough to be released from the hospital and Julia brought her home.

Julia's earlier experience as the parent of a child with reflux helped her in caring for Andrea, whose reflux increased in severity. She was already knowledgeable about the logistics of care and was able to manage Andrea's symptoms and keep her comfortable. Andrea also had a persistent cough and alarming rapid-breathing episodes. Trips to the doctor were frequent during her early months. It should be noted that Julia made the decision to adopt Andrea without really knowing much about what the future might hold in the way of health or developmental issues for her. She was, of course, concerned by the low APGAR score and the need for the CPAP, but says she never felt any doubt about going ahead with the adoption.

There were many similarities in the type of care Andrea and Morgan needed as infants, but there was a crucial difference in Julia's peace of mind as a parent. Julia had been able to meet both of Andrea's birth parents in the hospital, and they had voluntarily relinquished their parental rights before she took custody of the baby. Parenthood is always easier the second time around, and because Julia didn't have to worry that Andrea might be taken away, her babyhood was a breeze for Julia compared to Morgan's.

Julia has ongoing contact with Andrea's birth mother and regrets the fact that she was not able to make a similar arrangement with Morgan's birth family. Julia believes adopted children benefit from open and honest communication about their birth families and the circumstances of their adoptions, and she and Morgan have had painful but necessary conversations on this subject, with many more to come as Morgan's understanding increases. Julia will also have these conversations with Andrea, always guided by what she believes are her children's best interests.

One of the things Julia believes would be in her children's best interest is to have another sibling. She feels it would be especially good for Andrea to have a brother or sister close to her own age. Morgan is an absolutely wonderful sister, but she is much older than Andrea and will most likely be off to college when Andrea hasn't yet finished grade school. Julia started the search for a new brother or sister almost two years ago, and the process isn't going any better than it did the last time. Once again, she is feeling frustrated by the outrageous situations she has encountered while dealing with the various adoption "professionals" who say they can help her find a baby. My role in all of this is mostly to listen to her sad and frustrating stories and attempt to boost her spirits so she feels strong enough to keep trying. I wish I could do more to help.

Julia has been tenacious in her search for a child. She has contacted numerous agencies, facilitators, law centers, and attorneys and has followed every lead they have given her to its unsuccessful conclusion. She scours the various lists of "waiting children" posted by various agencies and regularly expresses interest in any child younger than Morgan, but something always prevents her from further consideration by the social workers who are making the decisions. The stories I'm now hearing from Julia are no more or less appalling than many of the other stories I've heard, but the sheer number of them has taken a toll on her.

Julia has been chosen twice by women working with an adoption facilitator and once by a woman working with an agency, only to have the placements fall through. The first time this happened, Julia was sad but not surprised. She had been contacted by the facilitator only three weeks before the baby was due and told that the family the woman had been working with had backed out at the last minute, with no further explanation. Julia was told that the woman was understandably hurt and angry, did not want to talk with any other adoptive parents, and just wanted the facilitator to handle everything for her. Julia felt terrible for her and also concerned about someone who would react to this situation by refusing to take further part in choosing her baby's adoptive family. To Julia, things didn't seem to add up, but the facilitator couldn't or wouldn't provide any further insight into the situation. This time Julia agreed to send the facilitator's fee of $6,000 and $1,200 for a month's living expenses. Then she waited, periodically checking in with the facilitator, who never had any additional information until a week after the due date when Julia was finally told the woman had decided not to proceed with the adoption. The facilitator explained that she would now present Julia's profile to other women and hopefully something would come up soon.

The same facilitator called about three weeks later to ask Julia if she wanted her profile to be presented to a woman who was newly pregnant, had four older children, and would need living expenses of $2,000 a month for at least seven months. Julia said yes and then had what she felt was a pleasant but confusing conversation with the woman, who talked happily about her children, describing each one and their various activities in great detail. But she expressed no interest in finding out anything more about Julia or her family. Julia's tactful attempts to find out something about the father of the baby were greeted with silence, and she was left feeling that other important information was being avoided as well. Most significantly, Julia could get no sense of the woman's reason for planning an adoption. She seemed to genuinely enjoy being a parent to her other children, and nothing in the conversation had shed any light on why she had decided she would not be able to raise this particular child. Obviously, money was a factor, but it wasn't the whole story.

Julia decided to put aside her concerns and try to get to know the woman better in the coming months. She offered to fly to the city where the woman lived so they could meet in person, thinking the woman would share her excitement at the prospect. But after several weeks of considering the idea, the woman decided she wasn't comfortable with a meeting. Julia arranged for a second phone call a few weeks later in which it became clear that the woman had no interest in talking with her. At this point Julia sought reassurance from the facilitator and was urged to just "hang in there" and try to understand that this woman was probably just "not a talker."

A few weeks later the facilitator called Julia to say that the woman needed some additional financial assistance. Her child support payment was late because her children's father had been laid off, she had missed work because the kids had been sick, and her car wasn't working so she couldn't take them to the doctor. Julia did send an additional $300 and then decided not to continue to provide financial support for this family. It was a hard decision, but Julia felt an immediate sense of relief not to be faced with another six months of worry and expense. She didn't want to be taken advantage of financially, and she didn't want to take on any emotional responsibility for the welfare of the other four children. And, most significantly, Julia continued to feel that this woman was unlikely to actually follow through with an adoption.

There followed a long dry spell in which Julia pursued leads but was never chosen by either pregnant women or the social workers who oversaw the placement of a child. Finally, she was contacted by an agency about a baby girl who was due in a month but whose mother's other babies had come early. Julia had a conversation with the woman, who seemed honest and forthcoming, and learned that this baby was going to be her third child. The older children had been adopted as infants by a paternal aunt. This baby had a different father, and his whereabouts, and even his name, were unknown to the woman. She was asking for nothing in the way of financial assistance and was eager to meet Julia.

Julia flew into action, knowing time was short, but not knowing just how short. A week later the agency called her to say that labor was going to be induced that night and Julia should get there as soon as possible. She scrambled to make immediate childcare arrangements for Morgan and Andrea and booked a red-eye flight to take her across the country. Julia was exhausted and anxious but, for some reason, felt confident that this time things would work out.

The expectant mother had been honest with Julia about her own intention to plan an adoption but had not anticipated the last-minute intervention of other family members. Often, extended family members who have stayed largely silent during the pregnancy and the planning stage of an adoption show up in force after the birth of the baby. It is perfectly understandable that these people want to protect and provide for their family, and it is usually in the child's best interest to be raised within their biological family. It is just sad that people like Julia and many, many other hopeful adoptive parents get so hurt in the process, simply because of a lack of communication and forethought within the birth family. Julia flew home without the baby and without much confidence in her ability to adopt a third child.

Parents like Julia are obviously invaluable to the children they adopt, and it should be obvious that they are invaluable to the rest of society as well. Julia is smart, and extremely determined, and I hope that she will succeed in building her family. She has shown over and over again that she is a wonderful parent. Morgan and Andrea have a mother who gives them an abundance of everything they need to thrive in life. Julia, and others like her, should be encouraged and assisted in their efforts to become parents; instead, the adoption process seems designed to thwart them. Thank goodness there are people like Julia who persevere, but surely even she has her limits.

CHAPTER NINE

~

Birth Mothers in the Media

Orphans abound in Western literature and mythology. From Moses to Orphan Annie, from Jane Eyre to Harry Potter, the plight of the orphan elicits sympathy, admiration, and idealization. Walt Disney, Shirley Temple, and a host of other entertainment figures have been frequent promoters of happy adoption stories. Their parentless main characters promote the archetypal orphan as a perfect combination of adorable, plucky, virtuous, self-sufficient, and endearing, with the clear message that such a fabulous child will inevitably find an equally wonderful family. These stories are meant to be inspiring and uplifting, and they usually succeed in that goal. But the image of adoption, as portrayed in the movies, has often had a distinct dark side, one that no doubt reflected the societal attitudes of their times. This is evident in the portrayal of birth and adoptive parents as natural enemies, fighting over a prize they couldn't both have. The battle lines between the two were always distinct, but which of them was the "bad guy" varied from movie to movie. Was it the lowlife birth parents versus the upstanding middle-class couple who longed for a baby? Or was it the coldhearted rich people versus the pregnant and struggling but also devoted and loving (and terribly repentant) young woman? Blood usually won out in these early movies, but occasionally a slatternly birth mother was sent packing or to her death so the child could thrive with more socially acceptable adoptive parents.

Birth parents were almost always shown to be either extremely good people who end up keeping their babies after fighting tremendous odds or bad or hapless people who eventually go away or conveniently die because of their own poor judgment. The only variation on these themes that I saw as a child was in the original version of the movie *Stella Dallas*, in which the title character, portrayed by Barbara Stanwyck, sacrifices her own happiness for the sake of her daughter. *Stella Dallas* is about a woman from the wrong side of the tracks whose vivacious spirit attracts the attention of the richest man in town. His family is not only rich—its members also all have hearts of gold. Sadly, fairly early in the marriage, Stella's rough-hewn ways make it impossible for the husband to stay with her, although he does continue to provide very nicely for Stella and their daughter, Laurel, who visits with him on holidays and during the summers. Laurel grows up to be a paragon of virtue who loves her mother dearly but also has a natural refinement (no doubt inherited from her father) that sometimes makes life in Stella's home awkward for her. Poor Stella and her boozy boyfriend just can't help being an embarrassment to Laurel as she gets older, though she's too refined ever to acknowledge negative feelings. After a series of difficulties, Stella decides that if she wants Laurel to have a good life, she will have to send her to live with her father and his new wife, a woman who is just as virtuous and refined as the daughter.

Stella pays a visit to the new wife and tells her that taking care of Laurel has become a burden and she wants to be free to pursue her own interests now that the girl is older. The new wife sees right through that story, but the two women nevertheless decide that it will be best for Laurel not to live with Stella anymore. Matters are further complicated when Laurel thinks she has figured out what Stella has done and tries to go back to her, only to be spurned. Presumably, Laurel quickly recovers from her mother's rejection and finds happiness in the life her father and his new wife can offer.

The final scene in the movie is of Laurel's marriage some years later, which is the society event of the season. The second wife has arranged for the ceremony to take place in front of a large window that opens onto a street, and she insists that the curtains remain open. The viewer understands that this kind woman suspects that Stella will be in the crowd of people outside, hoping to catch a glimpse of the bride. Sure enough, Stella˙ is there, and the last shot is of her tear-streaked face beaming with pride and the contented knowledge that she made the right decision to remove herself from Laurel's life—even as a policeman tells her to move along.

Among the many flaws in *Stella Dallas* is the message that being rich and refined is the best way to be—a widely held attitude in that era. It also is psychologically implausible, to say the least, that poor Laurel would suddenly and for no apparent reason be cast away by a mother who had previously been steadfastly devoted, and that such a devastating experience would take no terrible toll on the girl. But despite its flaws, this was the first movie I saw that suggested there could be a selfless reason (other than imminent danger, as in the story of Moses) for a modern-day woman to give up her child. Stella may have been misled by the values of the era, but there was no question that she loved her daughter and that her actions were motivated by that love. The movie also suggested that a woman would suffer for this decision, but if she had done it for the right reasons she would eventually find peace.

During the years I worked at the large adoption agency program, we spent a lot of time trying to come up with ways to spread the word about open adoption and to change negative perceptions about birth parents. Our counselors would go out to high schools to give presentations about adoption, and while students were interested in the subject in general, none of them ever seemed to imagine it as an option for themselves. We frequently heard the comment, "I couldn't do that to my child," voicing a widely held belief that children who had been adopted would always feel second-rate and would think their birth parents must not have loved them.

As soon as I started meeting birth parents, I could see that the perception of them as people who didn't care about their babies was completely false. They were people who cared enormously. It is not possible to be with a woman or girl who has just handed her newborn baby to adoptive parents and to not recognize the depth of her love and grief. The birth parents I worked with were enormously inspiring in their strength and sacrifice, and I wished there was a way to get this message across to the people who judged them harshly. Sadly, these people were often their families and peers—the people who had the greatest power to hurt them. I wished there was some way to spread the word about what was really going on when people made the decision to relinquish their babies. It seemed so clear to me that the truth about relinquishing a child, as lived by pretty much all the birth mothers I worked with, had all the elements of life's most poignant and compelling stories.

I used to fantasize about making a documentary about open adoption. It would start out with a close-up shot of a young woman's intense gaze, then slowly pan back to reveal that she was a pitcher in a softball game. As the camera continued to enlarge our view, the audience would see the woman's teammates, then the spectators, then eventually the whole stadium, making clear that this was a college game. The camera action would then reverse, finally focusing in on one person in the stands: a small boy, cheering wildly and waving. The final shot is of the pitcher again, smiling and waving back to the boy. Then the narration—the pitcher's voice—begins explaining what is happening.

I didn't work with this particular girl, but I remember when her story appeared on the evening news. She had gotten pregnant as a teenager and decided that adoption was the best choice for her baby. Though that in itself wasn't so unusual, what was remarkable about this girl was her decision to speak out about her experience with open adoption. She was proud of her child and of the decisions she had made for him, including the decision to have an ongoing relationship with his adoptive family. Her story was the perfect antidote to the widespread "I would never do that to my baby" attitude prevailing among high school kids. It was a fascinating story about personal triumph against odds and she was a compelling spokesperson for birth mothers.

Oddly, most people didn't seem to be all that interested in that part of her story. They were more intrigued by her status as an athlete than her status as a birth mother.

In 1989, with the appearance of the movie *Immediate Family*, Hollywood finally began to recognize some of the complexities and nuances of adoption. *Immediate Family* told the story of a privileged but infertile couple (Glenn Close and James Woods) who connect with a young pregnant woman (Mary Stuart Masterson) and plan an adoption. The film was realistic in some very important ways, with both the birth and adoptive parents presented as sympathetic characters deserving of good fortune. We get to know the adoptive parents a bit better than we do the birth parents, and the film is skewed to make you hope they adopt the baby, but the birth mother and birth father (Kevin Dillon) are extremely likable people who are shown to be loving and selfless when they ultimately decide to go through with the adoption. They are not presented as pitiable or irresponsible in any way. To my knowledge, this was a first in a mainstream Hollywood film.

The movie goes on to show the birth and adoptive parents genuinely caring about each other. In the final scene, we see Masterson busily at work; as she leans over to get something out of a drawer, we see that it holds a letter and a picture of the baby. She then leaves work and meets Dillon, and they go about their business in a seemingly happy way. Though it was an extremely painful sacrifice, we're led to believe they do not regret the adoption. Meanwhile, Close is shown cuddling the baby in his state-of-the art nursery. It's presented as a clearly win-win situation.

Admittedly, this is a Hollywood version of relinquishment. But at the time, it was a stunning breakthrough to render a positive depiction of adoption with what I felt was a more accurate portrayal of birth parents. My excitement over the film was dimmed in the months after its release, when *Immediate Family* didn't perform all that well at the box office (Masterson's Oscar nomination notwithstanding), and I didn't detect much in the way of change in societal attitudes toward birth mothers in the years that followed.

The change I yearned for finally arrived with the 2007 release of *Juno*. Not only was it sensitive in its portrayal of a birth mother, it also won an Academy Award for Best Screenplay (written by Diablo Cody) and nominations for Best Actress and Best Picture. Elliot Page plays the role of birth mother to perfection, playing (as had Masterson) a young woman who is smart, capable, and very independent. Neither of these birth mothers is presented as pathetic, reckless, or immoral. Though they are sad about the loss they are facing, they take charge of their situations and don't think of themselves as victims. Both characters clearly love their babies but feel that they cannot at that time in their lives be the parents they want their children to have. Because *Juno* attracted such a wide audience, the moviegoing public was educated about adoption in an unprecedented way.

In 2009, another huge step forward in the portrayal of birth parents was taken by the reality television show *16 and Pregnant*, when the show's most thoughtful and sympathetic teenaged couple, Catelynn and Tyler, decided on adoption for their baby. The audience followed along as they went through the decision-making process, and it was clear that this couple had their baby's best interests in mind every step of the way. Catelynn and Tyler were not only very young, they also came from dysfunctional families. Given their backgrounds, they were miraculously mature and realistic—far more so than average sixteen-year-olds. They could see from their own experience that their parents hadn't been able to provide stable homes for them when they were younger and couldn't be relied upon to help them with a baby now.

I was stunned one week to watch Tyler have the same argument with his father that I had seen played out repeatedly with young men I had known. Tyler's father objected to the idea of adoption and felt that Tyler should "man up" and take care of his child. The father berated him for not taking responsibility and said something about how he would never have given up on his own kid. Tyler, with the patience of Job, quietly reiterated that he felt adoption was the best choice and gracefully reminded his father that he had been in and out of jail and was frequently unavailable to Tyler throughout his childhood.

To the viewer, it seems clear that it is precisely because of the choices his father made that Tyler views adoption as a positive alternative. He sees his childhood as having been very difficult, he doesn't want his own child to face that sort of hardship, and he doesn't have the confidence that he, at age sixteen, can do better than his own father did as a parent. Catelynn's reasoning is similar, and they appear to be an amazing source of support and guidance for one another. All the other teenagers featured on the show decided to parent their babies and some of them tried to do it as couples, with varying degrees of drama and chaos and with all the couples who choose to parent ultimately breaking up.

Catelynn and Tyler are still together in 2022, married and with three more daughters. They have maintained an open relationship with their daughter's adoptive parents while being careful to preserve her privacy, which can't have been at all easy while they continued to take part in a reality TV show. These two still very young people not only handled their first child's adoption with remarkable thought and care, but they did the rest of us a huge service by letting us observe the process. Over time, we may well discover that things didn't always go as happily or as smoothly as everyone hoped they would. The fact that the sisters are being raised separately is a painful reminder of their ongoing loss, and Tyler, once again the poignant spokesman, summed things up with: "It sucks that we were so young."

I haven't worked with any pregnant teenagers since *16 and Pregnant* first aired who haven't been aware of Catelynn and Tyler, and the response to their story is overwhelmingly positive. I no longer do outreach at high schools, but I feel quite sure that because Catelynn and Tyler have so changed the public perception of adoption and of birth parents, discussion in schools these days would not as often begin and end with, "I'd never do that to my baby."

Early on, there was tremendous criticism of *16 and Pregnant* and its spin-off *Teen Mom*, which followed the young couples over their early years of adjusting to being parents. A vocal contingent of critics felt that the show glorified teenage pregnancy and parenthood. Fortunately, calmer heads prevailed as the hysterical outcry died down, and over time it became evident not only that these shows do the opposite of glorifying teen pregnancy and parenthood but also that there may be a direct correlation between their appearance and a recent decrease in teen pregnancy.

It has been encouraging to see signs of positive impact from these shows. People who track social media trends find tweets such as, "Just watched '16 and Pregnant.' Remembered to go take my birth control." The vast majority of teenage viewers are smart enough to know that if they were to get pregnant, there would be no television camera following them around. They understand that the girls and couples featured on the show have struggled mightily and that their lives as very young parents continue to be hard, despite their celebrity and some financial rewards for participating in the show. Of course, the participants love their children and no doubt feel that all the hardship was worth it in the end because of the children, but they don't mince words when it comes to advising other girls not to get pregnant. And those other girls—and their boyfriends—are apparently listening.

CHAPTER TEN

⁓

Did Birth Mothers Change?

Ironically, the enlightened portrayal of birth mothers in the media seems to have emerged just in time to be outdated, as changes in the adoption world brought about changes in the population of women who consider adoption for their babies. I'd had the sense that things were changing for a long time, but I hadn't properly examined the numbers until recently. A review of the infant adoptions I was involved with over the past twenty-five years yielded the following statistics:

1. In the twenty years between 1995 and 2015, fewer than 10 percent of the infant adoptions I worked on involved babies who tested positive for drugs at birth and/or whose birth mothers self-identified as drug users. Approximately 95 percent of these babies were adopted by biological relatives who were aware of the birth mother's history of substance abuse. But . . .

2. In the five years between 2015 and 2020, the percentage of infant adoptions I worked on that involved babies who tested positive for drugs at birth and/or whose birth mothers self-identified as drug users rose to 54 percent. Approximately 80 percent of these babies were adopted by nonrelatives. The adoptive parents were usually aware of the prenatal drug exposure prior to the placement of the

baby, but some felt uninformed about the full extent of the birth mother's use of drugs during the pregnancy.

3. In the twenty years between 1995 and 2015, I worked with only one birth mother who self-identified as homeless. But . . .

4. In the five years between 2015 and 2020, 15 percent of the infant adoptions I worked on involved birth mothers who self-identified as homeless.

These statistics speak to what is true for one counselor working with families adopting through a variety of agencies, facilitators, and attorneys, and they are eye-opening.

The most startling finding is the dramatic increase in just the past five years in the number of babies exposed to drugs in utero who are being adopted by people to whom they are not biologically related. It should be noted that my statistics reflect only situations in which women seek the assistance of an adoption professional, and I believe the majority of babies who are not being raised by their biological mothers are still being raised within their extended families without formalizing the relationship as a legal adoption. This is true regardless of the mother's use of drugs during pregnancy. It is clear that the United States has a huge drug problem, and that this has been the case for far longer than the past five years. The child welfare system has been dealing with its aftermath of child abuse and neglect for decades.

What my statistics most significantly reveal is not that there are more pregnant women using drugs, but that there are more nonrelative families who are interested in adopting the babies born to these women. What the statistics don't reveal is whether these families' relatively newfound comfort with prenatal drug exposure indicates increased knowledge (and a corresponding lack of concern) about the effects of drug exposure, increased desperation on the part of the adoptive parents, or both. I'm not sure the families themselves fully knew the answer to that question when they decided to go ahead with their adoptions.

During the first two decades of my career, almost all the families I worked with specified that they would not feel comfortable working with a pregnant woman who used drugs or alcohol during her pregnancy. In the early 2000s that stance was increasingly modified to reflect the realities of young adult life, which often included alcohol consumption and recreational drug use. Adoptive families began to realize that if they eliminated everyone who had engaged in this sort of partying, they would significantly reduce the number of people who might choose them as adoptive parents.

Families started specifying that they were open to situations in which a woman had used drugs or alcohol, but only prior to knowing that she was pregnant. They did not feel comfortable with a woman who would knowingly continue to endanger her baby, not only because of the potential for physical harm to the baby but because they did not want an ongoing relationship with someone who had a substance abuse problem. This position held steady for a long time, and it is still what families typically tell me during the home study process. But my statistics and experience indicate that somewhere between the home study and bringing home their babies, many of these families are changing their position on drug use.

The other statistic that is startling, and extremely dismaying, is the increase in the percentage of women self-identifying as homeless who are seeking the services of adoption professionals. One long-established and highly respected agency I work with has recently come to the attention of pregnant women in the homeless community in its city. Word has apparently spread that this agency will provide living expenses to pregnant women who are considering adoption. Suddenly the agency has found that this small but growing percentage of its clients is consuming the majority of its time and financial resources. The homeless women's pregnancies have all been high risk, primarily due to drug and alcohol use, mental health issues, and various untreated physical concerns. Some of these women have followed through with adoption, others have changed their minds about adoption after the birth, and there have been some scams. In looking ahead, the agency staff wonder how they can possibly continue to serve the needs of this extremely high-maintenance population.

The agency staff also have to ask themselves if their willingness to provide living expenses is encouraging homeless women to get pregnant when they otherwise would have avoided doing so. If the agency is to stay in business, it will have to pass along the extra cost-of-living expenses for these women to the adoptive parents, who will then be faced with a disproportionate financial burden. Which raises the question: Should the financial needs of the homeless, whether or not they are pregnant or are really considering adoption, be considered a reasonable adoption expense? Should the financial needs of pregnant women who are not homeless be considered a reasonable adoption expense? Reasonable or not, the majority of adoptive parents are now expected to provide this type of assistance.

Are the needs of these pregnant women greater than they used to be, or are the financial transactions in today's adoptions simply a reflection of what happens when only the laws of supply and demand dictate the way people act? I'm not an economist or a social scientist, and I'm sure there are multiple contributing factors, but I believe there has been a significant change in the population of pregnant women who consider adoption. The sheer number of women who are struggling with substance abuse, mental health problems and/or homelessness who have placed babies with the families I have worked with in just the past few years (a minuscule percentage of the total number of such women nationwide) forces me to draw this conclusion.

For most of my career there seemed to be a clear distinction between pregnant women who voluntarily relinquished their parental rights and those whose parental rights were involuntarily terminated by the state. Early in my career, I worked in the child welfare system and was familiar with the problems and challenges facing women whose children had been involuntarily taken into state custody and placed in foster homes. In contrast, as an adoption counselor, most of the women I knew who voluntarily sought the services of an adoption professional did not have the problems that would bring them to the attention of child protective services. For most of my clients the only significant distinction between them and their peers was the unplanned pregnancy. Like other adoption professionals, I could see that the women we worked with who were considering adoption for their babies were acting as loving and responsible parents who wanted their children to have lives they felt unable to provide. These women were struggling with an especially difficult and painful decision regarding adoption, but most weren't struggling with mental illness, drug addiction, or other overwhelming problems.

The women who did struggle with substance abuse or mental illness were far less likely to view adoption in a favorable light and far more likely to become clients of CPS. These women typically did not seek the help of adoption professionals and were unlikely to consider relinquishing their parental rights, even when they couldn't imagine being able raise the child themselves. Instead, the state would intervene at some point, sometimes even before the baby was released from the hospital, and the child would become part of the foster care system. The parents lost any sense of control over their own and their child's future.

In some cases there were happy outcomes where these women would actually benefit from state involvement and mandated services and would eventually regain custody of their children. But often, there was no happy outcome for anyone. The mothers would return to lives of dysfunction and the babies would spend years in foster care while the system tried to reunite the family. When that goal proved unattainable, the state would undertake the painful and lengthy process of terminating parental rights and freeing the children for adoption.

It's hard to determine just how and when it happened, but it now seems that some of the women who used to lose custody to the state have been drawn by promises of financial support to become the clients of adoption agencies, attorneys, and facilitators. In some ways this can be viewed as an encouraging development, since these voluntary relinquishments eliminate the need for foster care and result in babies going directly to their adoptive parents. But in important ways this can only be viewed as discouraging, further evidence of the erosion of the ethical standards that used to govern adoption.

I believe this change has come about not because women themselves are more troubled or less ethical than they used to be, but because a system that financially rewards them for producing babies is itself more troubled and less ethical. It seems astonishing to me that we have come to accept this practice as being in any way reasonable, yet somehow it is now acceptable to essentially pay women for their babies. It should not, then, surprise us that there are some women already living on the margins of society who might find this offer tempting. It also should not surprise us that the "living expenses" provided to birth mothers are almost always a significantly smaller percentage of the total cost of an adoption than the fees paid to either the agency, or the facilitator, or the attorney assisting with an adoption.

A well-functioning society should care for all its citizens, particularly those who are most in need of assistance. No one, and certainly not pregnant women and their unborn children, should suffer hunger or homelessness or be denied needed medical care. But we are not doing what we need to do as a society to address these issues, and countless people, including unborn babies, are suffering as a result. I believe it is the moral responsibility of every citizen to acknowledge this suffering along with the outrageous inequalities in income and opportunity that make it possible.

I also believe that a system in which individual adoptive parents are asked to temporarily ease the financial suffering of individual pregnant women whose babies they hope to adopt is not only unethical but actually serves to exacerbate the inequalities that exist between them. Pregnant women should have access to whatever financial help they need, whether or not they are considering adoption for their babies. And adoptive parents should not be forced into dubious financial arrangements, including bidding wars with other hopeful adoptive parents, in order to compete for those babies.

One of the most basic tenets, not only of ethical adoption but of an ethical society (at least since the abolition of slavery), is that people, including babies, cannot be bought or sold. Surely we can all agree that babies are not commodities and that birth parents should not be given money in exchange for their children, either as an incentive to relinquish their parental rights or as a reward for doing so. Pregnant women who need financial assistance should be guided to services and sources of support that are not influenced by or dependent upon the possibility of adoption. Telling ourselves, as adoption professionals and adoptive parents, that offers of financial assistance to a pregnant woman are motivated simply by the desire to provide care for her is disingenuous. Of course, we all do want the woman to be well cared for, but the only reason we have singled her out (as distinct from all the other pregnant women who need financial assistance) is because she has agreed to consider adoption, or at least pretend to be doing so. If we're honest with ourselves, we'll recognize this as a financial transaction.

CHAPTER ELEVEN

~

What Will We Tell the Children?

Adoption necessarily begins with sadness over the separation of a parent and child. There is no escaping that fact, nor is there anything to be gained in trying to convince ourselves or our children of anything different. I do not believe "everything happens as it should" or "there are no mistakes in life." I certainly believe that my own adopted daughter was destined to be my daughter, just as my birth children were destined to be my daughters. I do not think it was a mistake that the stars aligned perfectly to bring us all together, but I also understand that my adopted daughter's birth mother must feel entirely differently. Those same stars didn't align perfectly for her. This legacy of separation and loss is inherent in the creation of adoptive families.

I believe it is disrespectful to our children for adoptive parents to gloss over adoption's roots in loss and view it only from our own perspective of gain. In fact, I believe that acknowledging the sadness gives children permission to come to terms with it. Denying it can create a burdensome and unsustainable reality in which they feel responsible for their adoptive parents' happiness. It asks adoptees to embrace and preserve the belief that everything worked out for the best and ignores the reality that it wasn't necessarily the best for everyone. Recognizing adoption's roots in sadness is painful and emotionally complicated, but it is necessary and ultimately leads to understanding and acceptance not only of the circumstances of the adoption but the adoptees' own identity.

For most adoptive parents, talking with our children about adoption feels like a formidable responsibility. Fortunately, society has come a long way since the era of shame and secrecy that existed well into the 1990s (and still exists in some families), when many adoptive parents felt they shouldn't reveal the devastating news about adoption until a child was "old enough to handle the truth." The simple fact of adoption was considered problematic enough to justify avoiding honest discussions on the subject for as long as they could be avoided. For more than a few families, this approach created a core of dishonesty that negatively affected feelings of trust and security for both adoptive parents and adoptees.

It was an era in which counselors heard from worried and angry adoptive parents who were convinced their thirteen-year-old daughter's sudden rebellion was caused by the newfound knowledge that she had been adopted as a baby. Counselors also heard from worried and angry thirteen-year-olds who were convinced that their parents' previous silence on the subject of adoption meant that "my whole life has been a lie" and "I can't trust anything they tell me." Both parents and children in these situations felt bereft and feared they would never regain their secure and loving relationships. Fortunately, once they started communicating honestly with each other, most of them did.

The reforms in adoption that took root in the 1980s and eventually led to a widespread embrace of openness between birth and adoptive parents helped to eliminate the belief that secrecy somehow benefited anyone in the adoption triad. By the late 1990s, most adoptive parents recognized the importance of talking honestly with their children about adoption. The prevailing thought was that the subject could comfortably be introduced through photographs and children's books on adoption, sometimes even through books of photographs that had been created especially for a particular child. The idea was to present an age-appropriate introduction to the subject and handle the harder questions later. Adoptive parents gradually began using this approach and children responded well. These days, most children know that they were adopted long before they have any concept of what it actually means to have been adopted. Most importantly, their parents have been honest with them and have let them know that the door is open to future conversations on the subject, which can be initiated when the child is ready.

When open adoption and honest communication with children about adoption became normalized, the stories adoptive parents told their children about the circumstances of their adoptions changed dramatically. Whereas many adoptees (along with the rest of society) had previously been given the impression that their birth mothers were women and girls who had been somewhere on the scale between unlucky and immoral, openness created a very different stereotype. Now children were told that their birth mothers were the most loving and selfless people imaginable. They were so good that they had done the hardest thing a person could ever do and sacrificed their own happiness for the sake of their babies.

I know very well that most birth mothers are indeed loving and selfless, but this saintly characterization felt like an unrealistic backlash to the earlier, uncharitable images. It also seemed likely to be more than a bit confusing to children, especially when they were told that their birth mothers loved them so much that they had given them up. If their adoptive parents loved them that much too, might they also give them up? And how were children supposed to calmly accept the idea that they had been the beneficiaries of their birth mothers' suffering?

Underlying the extremes of presenting birth mothers as either sinners or saints was the basic dishonesty of treating them as a homogeneous group. Birth mothers are individuals, each bringing different circumstances to her adoption story. A few of them have, in fact, committed grievous sins, sometimes against their own children, and there are no doubt others who live exemplary lives. But most birth mothers are just like most other people, and this is what we should be telling our children about them. Adoptive parents will almost always do best by sticking to the facts of the matter rather than trying to create a story they think their child would like to hear.

Sadly, there are some birth mothers who have stories that will be very hard for adoptive parents to share honestly. How should adoptive parents handle conversations with their children when the circumstances of the adoption clearly indicate that it, and perhaps even the pregnancy itself, was financially motivated?

For the first thirty years of my career, I knew only a small number of women with unplanned pregnancies who placed more than one child for adoption. Repeat relinquishments were extremely rare, but in the past decade or so that has changed. These days I get contacted by adoption agencies, facilitators, and other individuals who are seeking adoptive families for women who are pregnant for the fifth, sixth, and seventh times. The record for one of these calls, for me, is an eleventh pregnancy. Sometimes these women are parenting a few of the children they have given birth to, but many of them have lost custody or have voluntarily placed those other children with relatives or adoptive families.

These situations are so familiar now that the "professionals" who are representing the women usually don't even bother to acknowledge the obvious dysfunction. Some of them actually say they believe "return birth mothers" are desirable clients because they "know what they are doing and are not going to change their minds about the adoption." While that statement is probably true and can be seen as expedient by both professionals and waiting adoptive parents, it overlooks the very disturbing question about why these women are seemingly deliberately becoming pregnant with babies they do not intend to parent.

One of my responsibilities as an adoption professional is to counsel adoptive parents about talking with their children about adoption. I'm supposed to stress the importance of creating an atmosphere in which information and attitudes are passed along in an open, honest, and respectful manner. The goal is to help the child feel secure in the knowledge that the adoption was handled lovingly and ethically and that both birth and adoptive parents, as well as any professionals involved, were always guided by the best interests of the child. Most birth and adoptive families these days embrace this goal, and even when there has been little contact between them, there is usually a basic respect and appreciation for the roles they each play in the child's life.

But how are parents supposed to openly, honestly, and lovingly pass on shocking and distressing information about the circumstances of their child's adoption? How will these children feel when they find out they were their birth mother's seventh child and the fourth one she relinquished for adoption? How will they feel about the amount of money that changed hands? Will they believe their birth parents and the adoption professionals really had their best interest at heart? My guess is that many of them are going to be shocked, hurt, and angry. I can only hope that it will be a well-placed anger and that it won't harm their relationships with either their birth or adoptive parents, because they are not the people to blame for this lamentable situation. Both the birth and the adoptive parents are pawns, as is the adoptee, in a much larger societal dysfunction. The blame should rest with a society that has allowed baby brokering to become an acceptable, largely ignorable response to poverty and desperation.

What will we tell all of our children about living in a society where it is a viable option to offer and accept money in exchange for a baby? What will we tell them about living in a society that refuses to fund social programs to support destitute and desperate pregnant women? What will we tell them about a society that leaves that responsibility to adoptive parents, who are desperate in their own way?

In the end I think we must return to the idea that children deserve to know these complicated and often very sad truths about the circumstances of their adoptions, as well as the truth about the societal problems that most likely led to those circumstances. This is the information they will need in order to call for adoption reforms that can benefit them, all of their parents, and all of society.

CHAPTER TWELVE

~

What about the Siblings?

Children who have been adopted often have biological siblings they don't live with and probably won't have the opportunity to know while they are young. In many cases, the children aren't even aware of their birth sibling's existence. Most commonly these are full or half siblings living with the shared biological parent or perhaps with another member of that extended family. They might also be half siblings who are living with a parent or extended family member who is not biologically related to the adoptee. There are also situations in which the adoptee has full or half siblings being raised by both of the biological parents. And there are situations in which full or half siblings are being raised in different adoptive homes or in the state foster care system.

In the past it was generally the case that children who had been adopted were not told about their biological siblings. Mercifully, that practice has become much less common, thanks to our understanding of the benefits of open adoption and honest communication. These days, adoptive parents usually tell our children about their siblings and tell ourselves that we will somehow be able to make the separation "okay" for them, even though they will have little to no contact as they grow up. It will be interesting, and probably quite sad, to hear what our children will have to say when they are older about how "okay" this really felt to them.

In this era of readily available genetic testing, it has become relatively easy to make contact with one's biological relatives, and many adult adoptees avail themselves of this opportunity. Some of them discover they have siblings and are eager to get to know them. While each situation is unique, there are two common stories we hear from siblings who were separated by adoption but have been able to meet as adults. One version expresses the idea that the adoptee was shocked but happy to have found out about the siblings, enjoyed meeting them, and is very grateful to have any information they can provide about the birth parents and family history. Further contact is anticipated but no specific plans have been made. After the initial excitement, they all settle back into their normal lives, maybe becoming Facebook friends who keep track of each other's lives but rarely see or speak with each other.

The second version is one in which the adoptee feels an immediate and strong connection to the siblings, who comfortably and enthusiastically embrace him or her as "one of them." These intense reunion stories are often tempered a bit over time as people come to terms with their different life experiences and perhaps with differing expectations for ongoing interaction, but loving relationships have been nurtured and are expected to continue.

These reunion stories are usually told by people who were unaware of each other while they were growing up, although there are also cases in which children who remained with the birth parent were aware of a sibling (usually the oldest or youngest in the family) who was adopted. Though sad that they were separated, these siblings typically express sympathy and understanding for the birth parents who made the painful decision to relinquish their child or children. This attitude of acceptance often extends to birth parents who lost custody due to substance abuse or mental health issues, and it even extends to parents who were extremely neglectful or abusive. Many of the children who have been adopted are infinitely forgiving, believing their birth parents were doing the best they could in extremely hard circumstances. Of course, there are also cases in which children who have been adopted feel hurt and angry at the birth parents and the circumstances surrounding their adoptions. Their long-held beliefs and attitudes about the adoption necessarily impact the sibling relationship.

Most people believe that siblings have a connection that runs deeper than shared physical traits or even a shared childhood. As it is when people who have been adopted meet their birth parents, separated siblings find commonality in surprising ways, such as in the way they speak or laugh, their sense of humor, their mannerisms, their talents and interests, and so on. Discovering these likenesses is fun and fascinating, but it can also intensify the sadness and loss they feel at having missed out on knowing each other as children and the knowledge that nothing they do now, as adults, can really make up for that lost time.

One of the saddest consequences of paying living expenses for expectant mothers considering adoption has been the emergence of a pattern of multiple relinquishments among financially desperate women. This is a trend that leads to an increase in the separation of biological siblings.

I recently worked with two families who adopted children who are now two years old and sixteen months old. Each adoption was handled by a different well-respected agency, each family provided living expenses to the birth mothers of their children, and each family had what they characterized as a good adoption experience, despite some significant challenges for one of them. In each of these cases, approximately one year after their first adoption, the families learned that their child's birth mother was pregnant again and that this baby would be their child's full biological sibling. At that point the stories diverge.

The first family, James and Sarah, worked with a large agency in another state and had limited but very meaningful contact with Caroline, their child's birth mother, during the pregnancy. She was the single mother of a young son and felt unable to provide for another child. She said she had met the father of the baby at a party but did not know his name or how to get in touch with him. The family was able to spend some time with Caroline in the hospital after the baby was born and they were impressed by her intelligence, maturity, and commitment to doing her best for both of her children. The baby was a beautiful little girl, Celia, who was soon displaying the sort of charisma and intelligence that drew everyone's attention. She was truly a sparkling personality and an absolute joy to her parents, her ten-year-old sister, and the entire extended family.

James and Sarah attempted to keep in touch with Caroline, but long periods of silence often followed their efforts. After one particularly long silence, Caroline contacted them to say that she was pregnant again and asked if they would be interested in adopting this baby, who would be Celia's full biological sibling. James and Sarah had definitely not planned to adopt another child. Celia was barely over one year old, they were both in their mid-forties, they had a child who was about to start middle school, and they hadn't financially prepared for another expensive adoption. But despite these practical considerations, James and Sarah soon realized they could not possibly pass up the opportunity to adopt this child and to raise Celia with her sibling.

James and Sarah feel enormously blessed to have been able to adopt Celia. The last thing they wanted to do was question Caroline's truthfulness, but the fact that this new baby was going to be a full sibling raised questions regarding Caroline's professed lack of knowledge about Celia's birth father. This time Caroline did give them the man's first name but insisted that she did not know how to contact him. As with Celia's adoption, the attorney would have to publish a legal notice for an unknown father for three weeks before the man's parental rights could be terminated. This was of concern legally, and James and Sarah were also concerned about not being able to provide the children with any information about their paternal heritage. However, Caroline remained steadfast in her assertion that she had no way of contacting this man, and there was nothing more James and Sarah or their attorney could do to clarify the situation.

As they had during Caroline's pregnancy with Celia, James and Sarah began paying for her monthly living expenses and happily anticipating the arrival of a baby boy. The wait was easier this time, but getting the new baby back home was enormously complicated by the fact that he was born in the first month of the COVID-19 pandemic and flying was dangerous. Fortunately, James had purchased some N95 masks several years earlier, during a particularly bad fire season in the Pacific Northwest, which helped them make the trip safely. The new baby, Parker, is only a few months old now and is just as sweet and enchanting as his big sister. The fact that they will be raised together makes this a joyful story with a happy ending for James and Sarah and their children.

But what if this isn't the end of the story? What if Caroline calls James and Sarah to tell them she is pregnant again? They certainly don't want to question Caroline's motives and choices. They want to assume only the best about her, but they are not naive. They are worried that Caroline's financial need and their willingness to pay for living expenses may have been the catalyst for the second pregnancy and might even be the catalyst for a third. They thought about discouraging another pregnancy by telling Caroline their family is now complete. But they don't know how to say that without being insulting, and if Caroline's pregnancies actually were financially motivated, wouldn't she just search for a different adoptive family if they were unavailable? That thought was also distressing and made James and Sarah realize they couldn't quite imagine saying no to Celia and Parker's full or half sibling. For now, they are focusing on the miracle of their two little children and trying not to dwell on "what ifs," the hardships Caroline faces, and the inequality between their lives and hers. James and Sarah are good people, trying their best to do the right thing for everyone.

James and Sarah's situation is still fairly unusual, but several weeks ago I got a call from another couple who had just learned that their son's birth mother is pregnant with a full sibling. Reid and Ben are a same-sex couple with two sons, both of whom were adopted at birth. Logan is now five years old and Carter is sixteen months old. It is Carter's birth mother who is expecting another baby, to be born in just three months. Reid and Ben's first adoption was handled by what they thought was a reputable agency, only to discover that it lost its license for various offenses shortly after Logan's placement.

When Logan was two and a half years old, Reid and Ben decided the time was right to adopt a second child. They went through several years of false starts and frustration before finally connecting with the agency working with Carter's birth mother, Elena. The agency was reaching outside of its pool of waiting families because Elena's situation was troubling and none of their regular families felt comfortable with the problems she presented.

The most frightening of the potential problems was that Elena was HIV positive and there was a possibility that it would be passed on to the baby. There was a high probability that even if the baby did test positive, he could be treated successfully. Nevertheless, though the prospect of dealing with this medical uncertainty was too much for most families, it was not too much for Reid and Ben. Barely ten minutes after my initial call to them and their quick conference with each other, they called back saying they were definitely interested.

It turned out that Elena had previously been connected to another family, one of the agency's regular clients, but they had decided against continuing to work with her as the difficulties mounted. The HIV status may have been what put them over the edge, but there had been other concerns as well, most notably Elena's drug use and apparent unwillingness to communicate with them. She and the baby's father, Chad, were living in a hotel that was initially paid for by the first adoptive family. Several weeks after they were officially chosen as the adoptive parents (and agreed to start paying living expenses and the agency fee), Reid and Ben traveled to meet Elena and Chad. They were distressed by obvious evidence of drug use, but after talking things over with several medical professionals, they decided they could handle whatever problems might arise. Reid and Ben were told that Elena had a teenage daughter who had entered the foster care system at age two and eventually been adopted, and that she also had an eight-year-old son who was currently in foster care. If Elena had not been planning an adoption, child protective services would be taking custody of this baby as well. Reid and Ben were determined to prevent that from happening.

Baby Carter was born about a month after Reid and Ben met Elena and Chad, and he did go through a period of withdrawal for about a week, as evidenced by his shaking and high-pitched crying. Mercifully, by the time they were able to bring him home, he was feeling much better. Carter quickly became a happy and healthy baby, described by his parents as "sweet, easygoing, inquisitive, and watchful." He was also very cuddly and spent much of his time sleeping on the chest of one or the other of his fathers. He ate well and grew so rapidly that his size, along with his glossy black hair and golden skin, led to speculation about possible Samoan heritage (speculation fueled by Chad's pronouncement that "this ain't my kid" upon seeing Carter for the first time). Carter is a beautiful baby and, like little Celia, has a personality that can light up the room. He is adored by his fathers, his big brother, and his extended family. He is not HIV positive and continues to thrive in all respects.

Reid and Ben have an open relationship with Logan's birth parents and various members of their extended families. Logan has always been aware that he has half brothers, who are eight, six, and four years old, and he has enjoyed a number of visits with them and other birth relatives over the years. Reid and Ben believe wholeheartedly in the benefits of open adoption and hoped to have the same sort of open relationship with Carter's birth parents, but Elena and Chad's drug use has made that complicated.

After they brought Carter home, Reid and Ben sent pictures and information to Elena and Chad in hopes that this would reassure them that he was doing well. When Carter was a month old, they made the five-hour drive back to the city where he was born in order to meet with his birth parents. The visit took place but was marred by obvious drug use and a simultaneous police raid on the hotel where Elena and Chad were living. Reid and Ben did not feel hopeful about the likelihood that either Elena or Chad could lead a drug-free life and explained to them that they weren't comfortable having further visits while they were still using drugs. At Elena's request, Reid and Ben did continue to send letters and pictures, via Elena's mother, and there were occasional phone calls. Unfortunately, Reid and Ben were never sure if Elena received the letters and pictures they sent since she and her mother "don't get along." (The mother, reasonably, didn't want to just give everything to Elena since she believed it would soon be lost or destroyed.)

When Carter was eleven months old, Ben got a call from Elena in which she hinted at the possibility that she might be pregnant again. She talked about the various courses of action she could take if it turned out to be true, none of them being that Reid and Ben would adopt this baby as well. Then five months passed without further word from Elena, despite overtures by Reid and Ben. When they did finally hear from her, they discovered that Elena was in fact pregnant, was due in three months with a baby who would be Carter's full sibling, and had already chosen a different adoptive family. Their first reaction was a sense of loss, for themselves and for Carter. But they realized pretty quickly that having a six-year-old and two babies under the age of nineteen months would stretch their limits as parents. And another costly adoption was out of reach for them financially.

Reid and Ben also realized that as much as they would have loved to raise this child, they couldn't imagine interfering with another family's adoption, particularly since this was going to be that family's first child. But they feel very strongly that Carter and the new baby should be able to get to know each other as children, and they are hopeful that the new adoptive family will share this view. Reid and Ben understand that this sort of contact between the adoptive families will also have to be approved by Elena or by the agency and they are prepared to be patient, even though the children are the ones who have most at stake.

Reid and Ben were amazed to find that Elena now sounds healthy and sober, and she informed them that she and Chad have been "clean" for the past six and seven months, respectively. This prompted Ben to ask if she wanted to arrange for a visit with Carter, but Elena declined, saying that she wanted to wait a bit longer because she didn't "want to be around him if I am using again," a terribly sad but pragmatic view. Reid and Ben are relieved that Elena is doing so much better now, but her current success also prompts the thought, "If only she could have done this when she was pregnant with Carter and spared him the suffering he went through." Now that Chad has put on some weight and is looking much healthier, the resemblance between him and Carter has become obvious. The children really will be full siblings.

In addition to his brother Logan and his yet-to-be-born full biological brother, baby Carter has two maternal half siblings and three paternal half siblings. None of these children is in the primary care of the shared birth parents. One of his maternal siblings lives with the maternal grandmother and the other has been in a foster home for about three years. The circumstances of the paternal half siblings are unknown to Reid and Ben. Logan has three maternal half siblings who live with his biological mother and one half sibling who lives with his biological father. That is a total of ten siblings, and it seems unlikely that even with the best of intentions, Reid and Ben could keep track of, let alone nurture, all these relationships. But they plan to try. Like James and Sarah, Reid and Ben are good people, trying to do their best for everyone, but it's complicated, to say the least.

~

CHAPTER THIRTEEN

John and Hannah

A Foster-to-Adopt Story

John and Hannah were in their midthirties when they met. Hannah, who had long known that she couldn't have biological children, had already been exploring the idea of adoption as a single parent. When, on one of their first dates, she told John about her plan, his shared enthusiasm thoroughly cemented the relationship, and they got married a year later. John and Hannah didn't have the money for either a private or an international adoption, but they had heard about their state's foster-to-adopt program and felt it would be a good way for them to become parents and provide a home for a child in need.

The process of getting licensed was long and complicated. Their training covered such areas as attachment theory, caring for drug-exposed infants, creating resilience after neglect and trauma, toddler adoption, relationships with birth parents, and a wide variety of subjects dealing with child development and parenting. There were also training sessions focused on the specifics of working with the Department of Children, Youth and Families and what foster parents could expect from the agency and the legal system after children were placed in their homes. By the time John and Hannah had completed the required training, they felt both overwhelmed by all the possible problems that might arise but also that they were as well prepared as they could be to handle them.

John and Hannah were conscientious students who learned their lessons well, but they actually had no intention of putting most of them to any practical use. They were requesting an infant and didn't expect that the child would have had time to experience too much trauma, and they only wanted to adopt a baby who was likely to be freed for adoption. They understood that the baby wouldn't be legally free for adoption at the time he or she was placed with them, but they wanted to be sure that the parents were unlikely to regain custody.

Not long after they were licensed, John and Hannah got a call about a baby boy named Luca whose mother was a seventeen-year-old girl who had used methamphetamines throughout most of her pregnancy. Luca, who weighed only three pounds, eleven ounces at birth, had been born drug affected, gone through withdrawal, and spent his first five weeks in the hospital. He now weighed seven pounds, his condition had stabilized, and he was ready to be placed in a foster home. Were they interested?

Yes, they replied. But what was the legal situation? How likely was it that Luca's mother would regain custody?

The caseworker explained that Aleena, Luca's mother, had left the hospital when he was only about eight hours old, at which point child protective services had been contacted. Aleena and the baby's father, Leon, who was ten years older, were living together at his mother's home, and all three of them were heavy drug users. No one answered the door at their house, and neither parent had responded to the caseworker's numerous phone messages asking them to contact her so they could make a plan for Luca. Of course, things could always change, and the state would need to give Aleena and Leon a chance, but it didn't appear that they were interested in parenting their son. They hadn't visited with him or even called to ask how Luca was doing during his entire hospital stay.

Heartbreaking as all this sounded, John and Hannah were encouraged. It seemed very unlikely that Luca would be returned to parents who had expressed no outward concern about their child. John and Hannah hadn't imagined that things would happen so fast, but the caseworker said that she needed to find a family who would be ready when Luca was released from the hospital in a few days. So they leapt into action, starting with a trip to Target accompanied by a friend who knew exactly what they'd need to buy. They then spent half the night setting up everything in the baby's room. John and Hannah dragged themselves into work the next morning to give their bosses the news that they would both be taking some time off. John planned to return to work after two weeks, and Hannah planned to stay home for six weeks. She wanted to make sure that the baby had fully adjusted to them before they introduced any additional caretakers into his life.

John and Hannah were excited, elated, and nervous (with a hint of terrified) the day before Luca's arrival. Exhausted from having slept so little the previous night, they went to bed early and woke up at 5:30 the next morning. There was an air of unreality to everything. They knew that they were about to take a step that would change their lives forever.

Luca was a beautiful baby with golden skin and soft black hair. He was sleeping in his car seat when the caseworker drove up but woke as he was carried into the house. Luca fussed for a moment but settled down immediately when Hannah offered him a bottle; then he fell asleep in her arms. Any thoughts about trying to preserve some emotional distance just in case he was taken away from them ceased to exist. Forty minutes later, when the caseworker left, John and Hannah were still staring in awe at the sleeping child.

For the first weeks, the adjustment to parenthood was a whirlwind of happiness and exhaustion, but soon life settled into a routine. Hannah loved being at home with Luca and extended her leave from six weeks to six months. She joined a new moms' group and made friends with other women in her neighborhood who had young children. The subject of Luca's foster child status was rarely mentioned, and the fact that he looked so much like Hannah, who shared his Latino heritage, gave people no reason to question whether he was her biological child.

The caseworker had explained to John and Hannah that she was required to try to work with Aleena and Leon before a permanent plan could be made regarding Luca's future. But it seemed obvious to John and Hannah that the caseworker would eventually be recommending them as adoptive parents.

But the wait was very, very hard. It got even harder seven months later when the caseworker told them that she was going to be moving on to a new job and Luca's case would soon be assigned to someone else. Another couple of months went by before the new caseworker informed them that he had finally been successful in connecting with Aleena. She and Leon had broken up, he had disappeared, and even his mother had no idea how to contact him. Aleena was now back at her own parents' home and had agreed to go to rehab. John and Hannah were terrified by the possibility of losing Luca and had to admit that they hoped Aleena would fail, and in a way she did. Over the next excruciating eleven months, Hannah took part in supervised visits with Aleena, where it became obvious to her that although Aleena loved her son, she had no ability to provide him with even the most basic care.

Aleena managed to stay clean for almost four months the first time, and plans were underway to allow her to have some unsupervised time with Luca, but then she relapsed. She got herself back into rehab after three months and had been clean for another four months when she revealed she was pregnant again. Aleena then made the decision to relinquish her parental rights to Luca and allow him to be adopted by John and Hannah if they would agree to an open adoption. She didn't think she could manage a baby and a two-year-old, but she wanted Luca and the new baby to know each other, so would John and Hannah agree to visits as long as she stayed clean?

By this point, they would have agreed to anything Aleena asked of them. Luca's adoption was finalized a month before his second birthday. John and Hannah kept in touch with Aleena and a visit was arranged so that he could meet his baby sister, Malia, when she was two months old. Shortly after that visit, Aleena moved in with a new boyfriend, and John and Hannah didn't hear from her again about future visits. This time they genuinely hoped that things would go well for Aleena, and at the same time, they couldn't help imagining the possibility that if they didn't, she would ask them to adopt Malia as well. But the months passed without any word from, or about, her. John and Hannah made it clear that they wanted to be contacted if Malia ever needed a home.

When Luca was three years old, John and Hannah decided it was time to think about adopting another child. Even though everything had worked out wonderfully for them in the end, they were afraid to try the foster-to-adopt route again. It had been enormously stressful for them, and the thought of exposing Luca to the possibility of losing a little brother or sister was terrifying. John and Hannah had been able to save some money over the past three years, so they decided to revisit the idea of doing a private adoption. When they contacted a local attorney who handled adoptions, he advised them to get their home study updated and then to post their profile on one of the websites for adoptive parents looking to connect with a birth mother. John and Hannah also contacted an adoption facilitator and an adoption law center to get information about how their services worked and felt optimistic about the information they received.

The first exciting phone call came about a month later when the facilitator called about a baby who was due in two months. The mother was committed to adoption and had already relinquished her parental rights to two other children, who had been adopted by different families. The father was unknown, and the facilitator would have to publish a legal notice for him, so this would be an "at-risk" placement. The facilitator's fee was $16,000, half of which was due when the mother chose a family and the other half when the baby was born. Living expenses for the mother would be low because she was due so soon and lived in subsidized housing. John and Hannah talked over the "at-risk" situation with their counselor and decided to proceed.

Hannah called the facilitator the next day to say that they would like their profile to be presented to this expectant mother. Hannah asked if the pregnancy had been confirmed; the facilitator said yes. But she then opened the file to check on something and "discovered" that the woman was expecting twins, a detail that had been overlooked in the previous conversation.

This was startling and exciting news and definitely required another conversation with John before going ahead. The facilitator told Hannah she could only give them a few more hours to decide what they wanted to do because she was going to present various family profiles to the woman that night. So Hannah and Luca showed up at John's office thirty minutes later and somehow everyone there got involved in deciding that John and Hannah definitely should become the parents of twins.

John and Hannah tried not to get their hopes up, but their minds were racing with thoughts about everything they would need to do to get ready for twins in just two months. The facilitator set up a call between Hannah and the pregnant woman, which took place a few days later and resulted in some more surprising news. The babies weren't due in two months, but in six months. Somehow that information had been recorded incorrectly in the initial intake information and had never been corrected. John and Hannah were just getting used to this new reality when the facilitator called to say that they had been chosen to be the adoptive parents. It was amazing news. So they sent the first $8,000 for the facilitator's fee, along with another $1,000 for miscellaneous expenses.

A week later, the facilitator called to say that the woman's subsidized housing had fallen through. Instead of minimal living expenses for two months, as John and Hannah had initially been told, she would now need substantial living expenses for six months. And they were reminded that the facililtator's fee didn't cover anything except making the match. From now on John and Hannah, who lived on the West Coast, and the expectant mother, on the East Coast, would need to work out any further details necessary to complete an adoption, and John and Hannah would need to hire attorneys in both states. It was turning out to be an expensive and risky situation in which they could spend a great deal of money and still end up without twin babies.

After much agonizing, they decided not to proceed. This was a bad introduction to private adoption, but at least the facilitator returned their money.

About four months later, Hannah thought she had found a possible connection to a pregnant woman through an adoption law center in another state. She knew someone who had successfully adopted through them, so she had sent in her information. The call she received was about a four-month-old girl whose mother wanted to plan an adoption because she didn't feel capable of taking care of her daughter any longer. The mother of the baby described herself as bipolar and said she had four older children, none of whom were living with her, though she didn't say why or offer any other information about their living situations.

After looking over John and Hannah's profile, the woman did choose them, and their excitement ramped up for a few days. Then Hannah was allowed to have a conversation with the baby's mother and the excitement promptly plummeted when the woman asked if Hannah would be "up for a fight" if the father objected to adoption. Further conversation revealed that the father hadn't even been told that the mother wanted to plan an adoption. The law center had apparently overlooked this particular legal detail, and their representative, who was on the line to monitor the conversation, attempted to downplay the problem.

Fortunately, Hannah knew enough about adoption to understand that a "fight" for this child was likely to be not only expensive but unethical and futile. There was no reason to assume that this man would, or should, agree to an adoption. The mother had made no effort to deny the father's interest in his child and even offered the information that he had recently taken the baby for an overnight visit. But she seemed to feel that a willingness to engage in a legal battle for the baby would be evidence of Hannah's strength and commitment as a parent. Hannah understood that the mother simply didn't understand how adoption law worked. But the woman from the law center should have known that this was likely to be a fight that would not end well for John and Hannah. After they told the woman that they would need more information about the father before they could consider proceeding, they never heard from the law center again: not about this baby or any other.

John and Hannah had had enough. They contacted their state caseworker and reactivated their foster home license. They told themselves that things would probably go more smoothly this time and that nothing could possibly be worse than the stress they had endured when they thought they were going to lose Luca. Three months later, the caseworker called them about a six-month-old baby girl named Ariana. Like Luca, she had been born drug affected, but unlike Luca, she had been allowed to go home with her mother, under supervision from CPS. Things seemed to be going well for the first few months, but the pediatrician had ongoing concerns about her low weight gain, and by the time of her four-month checkup there were concerns that Ariana was not meeting developmental milestones. Home visits from a feeding specialist and physical therapist were initiated, but after a few weeks both of these people reported that the mother, Krista, seemed unable to make use of their assistance.

The pediatrician and caseworker felt the situation warranted place-ment in a therapeutic foster home, and that was where Ariana had been for the past six weeks. She had put on weight almost immediately. Meanwhile, Krista had declined to visit with Ariana or to engage with the caseworker in any way. She also had three older children who had been removed from her care several years earlier by CPS. The two oldest were now living with their father, and the other child, who had a different father, was with a paternal aunt. Krista said that Ariana's father was a man whose name and whereabouts she did not know and that there was no one in her own family who would provide for her kids.

It seemed to John and Hannah that after failing to regain custody of any of her other children, Krista probably wouldn't suddenly be capable of parenting Ariana. They knew the state would have to give Krista time and that there would be a period of risk for them, but they felt better able to handle the uncertainty now that they were already parents. Nevertheless, they worried about the impact that both Ariana's arrival and her possible departure would have on Luca, who was now four years old.

John and Hannah expected that Luca would go through a period of adjustment, as kids generally do when a new baby joins the family. They thought he might feel anxious and jealous of the attention Ariana required. But Luca was thrilled with Ariana. The fact that she was a quiet baby who rarely cried or fussed and almost always slept well through the night made their adjustment to each other pretty smooth. That Luca was the first one in the family to get Ariana to smile made him feel extra important, as indeed he was.

Ariana was an easy baby to take care of and generally seemed content to watch whatever was happening around her. She would sit in her car seat or on a blanket on the floor, seemingly happy, until she got tired and fell asleep. She didn't fuss when they put her to bed at night and she didn't fuss when she woke up in the morning. After her first night with them, John and Hannah thought Ariana must just be very good sleeper, but when they peeked in the next morning and saw her lying quietly in her crib, they realized that she could have been awake for hours. Yes, she was an "easy" baby—but for all the wrong reasons. Ariana had given up on the idea that her fussing, or the fact that she was hungry or tired or lonely, mattered to anyone. She didn't fuss because she didn't expect anyone to respond.

John and Hannah revised any previous opinions they had had about the proper approach to baby care. They moved her crib into their room, and they often moved her into their bed, and responded to every little sound she made. Fortunately Ariana was still a good sleeper and didn't wake often, but when she did they were right there to reassure her. At nap time and bedtime she would fall asleep in someone's arms before being put into her crib, and when the family went out, Ariana was in a baby carrier rather than a stroller. Her lightweight status made this easy for both John and Hannah until she was almost a year old. At that point Ariana started to show an interest in moving around when she was placed on the floor, and within another four months she was reaching normal developmental milestones.

At first, John and Hannah wondered if Ariana's passivity might also be evidence of a very easygoing nature, but as soon as she started to scoot around the floor, Ariana began displaying all sorts of opinions and tenacity. She knew exactly what toy she wanted and where she wanted to go, and nothing was going to stop her. John and Hannah and Luca loved her and loved watching her personality emerge. Ariana now always called for someone the minute she woke up in the mornings or from her nap, so they moved her back into her own room. She still fell asleep in their arms, but this was something John and Hannah probably enjoyed even more than Ariana did, so no one was eager to make a change. Luca continued to be an amazing big brother, and it was obvious that the children adored each other.

Krista resisted all efforts at communication from the caseworker regarding Ariana until she received notification that a court date had been set to terminate her parental rights. This finally spurred her into action to delay that process. Krista met with her attorney and was persuaded to tell the judge that she would enter a three-month drug treatment program, which she did when Ariana was fifteen months old. Much to everyone's surprise, Krista successfully completed the program. She then moved to a sober house and started working at a grocery store. As they had been when it seemed that Aleena might regain custody of Luca, John and Hannah were terrified at the prospect of losing Ariana.

When Ariana was eighteen months old and Krista had completed rehab, the caseworker decided that it was time to institute supervised visitation. Hannah was asked to bring her to the DCFS office, stay with her until she felt Ariana had adjusted to the new faces (of Krista and the caseworker), and then leave them alone for a while. She could stay within earshot and return if Ariana showed any sign of distress. Mercifully, Ariana didn't become distressed during the twenty-minute visit, but Hannah was entirely distraught.

Hannah was required to take Ariana for two more visits. But then there was a seven-month period in which Krista relapsed twice before disappearing. Ultimately, the state terminated Krista's parental rights, an action that had seemed necessary when Ariana first came into care but didn't happen until she was almost three years old. Was all the struggle John and Hannah had gone through worth it? Obviously. But would they recommend the foster-to-adopt program to someone else? Not so obvious.

CHAPTER FOURTEEN

~

What about All the Kids in Foster Care?

I used to know a number of adoptive parents who were active in an adoptive parent support group connected to a large agency where I worked. The agency handled international adoptions as well as domestic infant adoptions and older child placements, and all the families who adopted through them were encouraged to join the adoptive parent support group in their area. The parents who were most active in my local support group were those who had children who did not share their racial heritage and/or were not infants at the time of the adoptive placement. Some support group members at the time assumed that the families who had adopted same-race infants didn't join the support groups because they felt no need for ongoing support. There was also some suspicion that these people wished to (and could, because their children shared their racial heritage) distance themselves and their children from the subject of adoption.

There was a lack of empathy for the families adopting same-race infants, and though it was ostensibly good-humored, there was definitely implied criticism when some members of the support group referred to the white infants as "plain white babies." Counselors were urged to try to encourage new adoptive applicants to "open their hearts" to the plight of an older child or a child with special needs.

Families who did adopt this sort of child (and sometimes many more children) were definitely the rock stars of the agency. Their status was well deserved.

But the disdain some people directed at families who wanted to adopt a same-race infant was not only undeserved, it was unkind. This same sort of implied criticism exists when uninformed people question prospective adoptive parents about why they insist on adopting an infant when there are so many children in foster care who need homes. Yes, there are many, many wonderful children in foster care, but they are not legally free for adoption when they come into care. This means that families who want to adopt can either take a child into their home who may ultimately be taken away, or they can adopt an older child whose parental rights have already been terminated. But terminating parental rights is a process that can go on for years, and these are not years in which the child is likely to thrive while peacefully and happily waiting for his or her adoptive family. Instead, he or she is likely to experience multiple caretakers, insecure attachments, increased risk of neglect or abuse, and other traumas inherent to the foster care system despite ongoing efforts at reform.

People feel called to become foster parents for all sorts of good and noble reasons. People feel called to become adoptive parents of an infant because they want a child—the same reason people become pregnant, and there is nothing necessarily noble about it. The motives of foster and adoptive parents should not be confused. The reason they have gotten confused in recent years is that due to the difficulty and expense of adopting an infant privately or through an agency, some adoptive parents have turned to the foster care system in hopes of finding an infant to adopt. These people were encouraged by the widespread initiation of the foster-to-adopt system, in which infants who come into foster care and are identified by their caseworkers as unlikely to be reunited with their birth parents are placed in prospective adoptive homes rather than regular foster homes.

The impetus behind the foster-to-adopt program was the (correct) belief that it would allow the child to develop bonds with prospective adoptive parents rather than with foster parents who were unlikely to become their adoptive parents. It was initiated in response to old (and now reviled) policies in which foster parents were not allowed to adopt the children in their care. These policies arose from a misguided effort to discourage foster parents from bonding with the children in their care and being tempted to subvert the goal of reunification with the biological parents. It was an especially cruel system that stayed in place for decades despite the obvious harm it caused—particularly to the children who were forced to leave long-term, loving foster homes in order to adhere to state adoption policy. However, it should be acknowledged that this sort of subversion of reunification efforts on the part of foster parents continues to be a problem for the foster care system.

Foster-to-adopt programs were an appealing alternative to expensive agency or private adoption, and plenty of hopeful adoptive parents jumped at the opportunity. For many of them things eventually worked out, if not quickly or easily. But some other families and children did not fare well at all. The statistics of the foster-to-adopt program probably look reasonably good, but the problem with statistics in such a high-stakes situation is that if you are on the losing end, it is 100 percent devastating.

In theory, I am a proponent of the foster-to-adopt concept and the idea that the child's best interests take precedence over every other consideration. It seems clearly better to allow an infant to develop bonds with the people who are likely to become his or her parents, even if there is an element of uncertainty about the security of the placement. Surely the adults, rather than the infant, will be better able to handle the risk and possible loss if they are eventually separated. But we need to think carefully about who these foster-to-adopt parents are and what we are asking not only of them but of the children.

My knowledge of the foster-to-adopt system is skewed by the fact that the families I hear from directly are those who have had bad experiences. In most cases, if a family had been able to foster-to-adopt successfully, they would not be contacting me at all. The ones who do so are likely to be those who ultimately lost a child they had hoped and expected to be able to adopt. I have also worked with families who did manage to adopt their children through the foster-to-adopt system but found the process so traumatic that they would not recommend it to anyone else.

Consider the story of Ben and Ellie. They married when they were in their late twenties and five months later were excitedly expecting their first child. Ben had started his own construction business three years earlier, and Ellie worked as his office manager. They had every expectation that the business would succeed, but it was still in the very early stages, so money was tight. Sadly, Ellie miscarried at the end of the first trimester. She was pregnant again within a few months and then miscarried a second time. Ben and Ellie were crushed by each loss. Although people kept telling her that this was all normal and they should just keep trying, after a third miscarriage Ellie sought the help of an infertility specialist. It was a difficult step to take, since they had no insurance and very little money, but she and Ben were more than willing to take on considerable debt in order to have a child. They quickly concluded that the doctor was worth every bit of the expense because he was able to diagnose the problem and recommend a relatively safe and easy procedure that could help Ellie carry a pregnancy to term. Ellie did become pregnant again and this time she gave birth prematurely to a baby boy, Cooper, who weighed 2 pounds, 6 ounces and lived for only five days. Ben and Ellie were always at his side, holding his tiny hand through the openings in the isolette and praying for him to hang on. Their grief seemed bottomless.

It was almost three years before Ellie could even think about having a child again. But she couldn't imagine risking the loss of a fifth baby. So the idea of adopting a child began to appeal to her. With adoption they would know that the baby was alive and healthy before they even met him or her and became attached. It seemed a much safer approach for them to take than another pregnancy. Ben and Ellie also liked the idea of adopting a baby who needed parents and the idea that the three of them could fulfill each other's need for a family.

After doing a little research, Ben and Ellie discovered that it was much harder to adopt a baby than they had expected—and also far, far more expensive. They still had a mountain of medical bills to pay off. Their business was going fairly well, but there is always a degree of financial uncertainty in being self-employed, and they really couldn't take on any more debt. They decided to check into the foster care system through the Department of Children, Youth and Families and discovered the foster-to-adopt program.

Over the next four months, Ben and Ellie took the required education classes, then went through the home study process, and finally were licensed as foster parents. They made it clear every step of the way that they wanted to adopt and were only interested in fostering an infant who was going to become available for adoption. They were told that they would be contacted about babies only when the caseworker was "planning to move to termination" and also that they would always be the ultimate decision makers as to whether a given child was placed with them. Of course, Ben and Ellie were also told that the caseworkers couldn't predict the future and that there had been cases in which babies were placed in prospective adoptive homes and then removed when the birth parent or another relative was able to regain custody. Ben and Ellie understood that birth parents and relatives would—and, in most cases, should—have priority over foster-to-adopt parents. They just wanted to be careful to avoid situations in which that seemed likely.

Two months after they were licensed, Ben and Ellie received a call about a baby girl. She was still in the hospital and was going through withdrawal, having been born to a mother who had used meth late in the pregnancy. The baby was this woman's third child; the other two, who were two and three years old, were in the custody of the paternal grandmother. This baby had a different father, and the grandmother said she had her hands full and was not interested in taking on another child, especially one to whom she was not biologically related.

The caseworker explained to Ben and Ellie that she felt there was minimal risk that the mother or father would regain custody of this child. The woman had left the hospital just hours after delivering, against doctor's orders, and had not asked to see the baby. Apparently her behavior had been similar at the births of her other children, each of whom had also been born drug affected and were placed with the grandmother at birth. The father of the older children hadn't been in contact with his mother or the children in years. The caseworker said the mother was unclear about who the father of the new baby was and definitely wouldn't know how to locate him. It did indeed, as the caseworker said, seem safe to assume that this was a case in which the parents' rights would be terminated and the baby would become eligible for adoption.

Ben and Ellie flew into action, gathering up the various baby items they would need and telling their families the exciting news. Two days later they drove to the hospital and came home with an adorable two-week-old baby girl who no longer showed any signs of withdrawal.

She was a dream baby who seemed to easily adapt to whatever was happening around her. She went to sleep peacefully, woke up happily, was easily comforted, and soon responded to their voices and their touch. Within just a few weeks she started to smile and make happy noises when they talked to her. Her name was Ava, and Ben and Ellie had never been so happy in their lives.

This was the lovely state they lived in for almost a year. Ava thrived in every respect, and so did Ben and Ellie. Visits from the caseworker were infrequent, which seemed fine, and whenever Ellie worked up the nerve to ask about Ava's mother, she was told that there had been no contact, which seemed more than fine. But what Ben and Ellie did not think to ask was if there had been any contact with other family members.

It wasn't until two days before Ava's first birthday that Ben and Ellie discovered that the grandmother of the other children had had a change of heart. She apparently now felt that the three children should be kept together and that Ava had a right to be raised with her half siblings. The grandmother was getting ready to finalize the adoption of the older children and wanted to know if she could adopt Ava as well. The caseworker explained to Ben and Ellie that the state did have a preference for placing children with relatives, even half siblings, whenever possible. They also needed to consider the fact that the children were all biracial, as was the grandmother, while Ben and Ellie were white. The caseworker felt that it would be better for Ava to grow up in a family that shared her racial heritage. It was extremely regrettable that the grandmother had waited so long to come forward, but the caseworker determined this did not negate the long-term benefits of Ava's being raised with biological family members.

So Ben and Ellie were forced to hand over a baby whose eyes lit up and whole body wriggled in delight when they came into her room in the morning, a baby who had just started to call them Mama and Dada with authority. The caseworker had explained ahead of time that she would arrange for some visits in which Ava could get to know the grandmother, but after that she thought it would be best to make the break as quickly as possible. Ben and Ellie had numbly agreed, but when the caseworker reached for her and Ava turned away and buried her face in Ellie's neck, they knew they had been wrong. There would be nothing "best" about this process, and the depth of their grief was magnified exponentially by the knowledge that Ava was grieving for them as well.

Ben and Ellie were playing the odds when Ava was placed in their home. They thought there was a good chance that they would be among the families who completed successful adoptions through the foster-to-adopt program, and even though they knew there was an element of risk, they saw no other path toward their dream of becoming the parents of an infant.

Wanting a baby was not an unreasonable dream. Nor was it unreasonable to expect that things could work out as they hoped. And it was certainly not unreasonable to put their faith in the idea that after all they had suffered, surely their luck would at some point have to change. But it did not. And Ben and Ellie have concluded that it never will. They have stopped searching for a baby to adopt and can't imagine how they would react if the opportunity somehow arose again for them. They would want to say yes and hope that loving that child would heal them, but they both believe it is too late for that. They feel irretrievably damaged, as though their hearts have hardened into defensive positions that can no longer stretch to embrace any child.

CHAPTER FIFTEEN

~

Working with the
Child Welfare System

The eye-opening early years of my career were spent working in the foster care unit of the Michigan Department of Social Services. I've written about those years in *The Children Money Can Buy*, so suffice it to say that I formed strong opinions about state child welfare systems. I remain both horrified by their failings and in grateful awe of the professionals who work so hard to navigate them successfully. My criticism of the ways the state child welfare systems interact with both private and agency adoption systems is not directed at individual caseworkers, though there are some who deserve not just criticism but censure. My complaint is about a lack of awareness within the state systems that works in opposition to parents' rights to make adoption decisions for their own children.

A number of years ago, I received an evening call from a doctor who advised me that she was working with Maddie, a seventeen-year-old girl who was going to be giving birth in a few weeks and wanted to plan an adoption. The girl's stepfather was the father of the baby. The following day the doctor called to report that the baby had been born early, at home. He and Maddie had been taken by ambulance to the hospital, where the baby would remain for observation because of the circumstances of his delivery, but Maddie had declined to stay. I arranged to travel to the town where she lived and meet with Maddie the following day. Shortly before that meeting I got a call from the child protective services caseworker who had been assigned to investigate the case, probably after referrals from the doctor and the hospital. I explained to her that I hadn't yet talked with Maddie, but that I would get back in touch with her after doing so.

A quiet and articulate girl, Maddie was absolutely certain she wanted her baby to be adopted. There was a toddler at the house as well, and it turned out that Maddie had given birth to him at age fifteen. The stepfather was not the biological father of that child. During that pregnancy, Maddie had worked with another adoption agency and had planned to place the baby with an adoptive family but had been prevented from doing so at the last minute by her mother. That baby had eventually been adopted by Maddie's mother and stepfather, and she was adamant that she did not want the same thing to happen to her second baby. She was afraid her mother would somehow prevent this adoption as well, and she was afraid of her mother's reaction if and when she discovered that her husband was the baby's father. Maddie told me she could stay with an aunt if necessary but, despite everything, she felt that her home was safe.

Maddie's focus was not on herself, but on getting the baby to an adoptive home. So we talked about open adoption, and she carefully considered all the family profiles I had brought, from which she chose a family. But she did not feel ready to meet them quite yet. I explained that I would have to talk with her stepfather as well, and Maddie assured me that he would agree to an adoption. I asked if I could assist her in the conversation with her mother, but Maddie didn't feel ready for that either. She knew it would have to happen, but she needed some time to gather her strength. It was, after all, only two days since she had given birth.

As I left, I told Maddie that I would get in touch with the attorney and that, because she was under eighteen, she would also need to meet with a guardian ad litem, whose role would be to represent her legal interests, make sure she was fully informed, and make sure that she was not being pressured by anyone to relinquish her child.

Before leaving town, I updated Margaret, her CPS worker, on my meeting with Maddie and arranged to meet with her when I returned. There was no sign of any difficulty during that call, nor at the meeting with Margaret the following day. I asked if she wanted to accompany me when I met with the birth father that evening, but she declined. Instead she met with Maddie and her mother and broke the news about the stepfather's paternity and the pending adoption. According to Maddie, Margaret told them she felt very strongly that Maddie's mother should have a decision-making role in this adoption and had even cried while recounting a story from her own life in which she had felt powerless when her teenage daughter's doctor had refused to disclose confidential medical information. Margaret felt this had been morally wrong and urged Maddie's mother to agree that parents should maintain authority over their minor children. Instead, both Maddie and her mother felt that Margaret had acted very inappropriately in trying to pressure them to see things her way.

Thankfully, Margaret's intervention did open up the conversation between Maddie and her mother, who told the stepfather to pack his bags, though it was unclear how long he would actually stay away. Maddie's mother decided that she would support the adoption this time if that was what Maddie wanted. My meeting with the step-father was uneventful. He was extremely eager to sign his consent, probably hoping that this would absolve him not only of any responsibility for the baby but also of any responsibility for his illegal sexual relationship with Maddie.

Maddie was extremely relieved by her mother's response and buoyed by her support. She was also relieved and happy to know that the baby, who was now three days old, could soon be with his adoptive parents. Maddie met with the guardian ad litem, and all the necessary paperwork was in place for an adoption. Maddie and her mother had a last visit with the baby the night before he was to be released from the hospital, comforted by thoughts of the happiness and security he would have with his adoptive parents.

Arriving at the hospital the next day, the adoptive parents expected to meet their baby boy but instead were told that CPS had placed a "hold" on the baby. Despite the court order giving the adoptive parents legal custody, they could not even see the baby, let alone take him home.

It turned out that Margaret had decided to simply overlook the legalities (including the fact that no pending dependency case had been filed for either Maddie or the baby) and to assert that she had "more power than the superior court judge" who had reviewed the guardian ad litem's report and entered an order establishing custody and guardianship and directing the hospital to release the baby to his adoptive parents.

The family's attorney had a bizarre conversation with Margaret in which she insisted that she could not be forced to release her hold on the baby. She first claimed that he needed to stay in the hospital for medical reasons (despite the fact that the hospital was saying otherwise), then claimed that she couldn't be sure that the people who claimed to be the adoptive parents were really who they said they were. Throughout the conversation, she stressed both her ultimate power and the fact that she was "just protecting babies." Things came to a tense end when the attorney convinced Margaret to discuss the situation with her own supervisor, who then promptly released the hold. The whole thing took only a few extra hours, but they were agonizing hours for the adoptive parents and a traumatic introduction to parenthood. Happily, everything went smoothly after that for both the birth and adoptive families, who finally met when the baby was a month old.

Margaret continued to cause difficulties, though, finding it necessary to attempt retribution by accusing me (a mandatory reporter) of failing to make a CPS report. The fact that I had already spoken with Margaret and knew that CPS was involved in the case before ever speaking with Maddie didn't dissuade her from filing a formal complaint. Although it went nowhere, it necessitated the involvement of an attorney to assure that the charge didn't affect my agency license. The family's attorney wrote a letter of complaint to the attorney general about Margaret's overreaching and the need for additional training for CPS staff about legal authority. I'm sure neither the attorney, nor I, nor the adoptive family expected a satisfying response from the state, and none came.

It is this lack of response and accountability that makes working with the Department of Children, Youth and Families so frustrating and discouraging. It is not the failure of Margaret, or any other caseworker, to act professionally, it is the failure of DCYF to create and support a system in which caseworkers understand that they can work collaboratively with adoption professionals. We are not working at cross-purposes; there should be no need for power plays or confusion about how best to "protect babies."

I have deliberately chosen a very simple and straightforward example to illustrate the problems that can arise when the foster care and adoption systems both work with women who are planning an adoption for their babies. Most of the time when CPS is involved, the situations are enormously complex. They often involve women who have a history of child abuse or neglect and whose other children are currently in the foster care system. These women have been told that the state ultimately will take custody of the new baby, too, so they have decided to plan an adoption so that they, instead of some caseworker they already don't like, will be the one to make decisions about their baby's future. At the very least, these women want to choose the adoptive family and arrange to have ongoing contact. These situations are often greatly complicated by the woman's history of substance abuse or mental health concerns. There is nothing straightforward about them and they are rarely resolved in a timely manner, whether by restoring parental custody or by terminating parental rights and freeing the children for adoption.

I am fully aware of the enormity of the task that state caseworkers face, both emotionally and logistically, and I have no desire to minimize their efforts or their commitment to doing what they believe is in the best interest of their clients. Caseworkers who work for the state have a mandated goal of reuniting the families whose children they have placed in foster care. The majority of their clients share this goal, but occasionally there are clients like Maddie, who want to plan an adoption. It should be possible for CPS workers and adoption professionals to work together with a clear understanding and appreciation for each other's roles and responsibilities. Presumably, in these cases, they are both working to further the client's goal of an adoption within the legal and ethical frameworks guiding adoption practice.

So what is preventing them from collaborating cooperatively? I think the first problem is that caseworkers like Margaret are suspicious when everything seems to be moving too quickly and people are challenging their authority. They want to slow things down so they can assess the situation and have some time to develop a well-thought-out plan for the baby. And, of course, they also have a caseload full of other clients and don't have the luxury of putting the needs of those people on hold in order to focus on one particular child. They feel that putting the baby in a foster home for a week or so will give everyone time to figure out how best to proceed. They do not necessarily share the urgency of the birth and adoptive parents' desire to avoid any foster care placement and have the baby placed with the adoptive parents directly from the hospital.

Another problem is that the caseworkers may have no information about the credentials of the agency, attorney, or facilitator handling the adoption. This should not be an issue when an adoption is being handled (as in Maddie's case) by an adoption agency that is licensed and overseen by DCYF. But caseworkers may also find themselves asked to work with out-of-state agencies, adoption facilitators, and attorneys they have no knowledge of and whose credentials they have no way of assessing. It is therefore understandable that they would feel anxious in these situations and want to take whatever time is necessary to assure that ethical standards are being upheld.

It seems unreasonable and impractical to ask that in addition to all their other responsibilities, individual CPS caseworkers be knowledge-able about every aspect of adoption practice. It also seems unreasonable to expect them to be able to research the credentials of all the various adoption practitioners they may encounter. So I would suggest that a system be established that relieves CPS workers of this extra respon-sibility and creates a source of referrals to trusted adoption profes-sionals when a CPS client is considering adoption. These adoption specialists could be individuals affiliated with agencies licensed by DCYF or otherwise accredited by the state. In addition to understanding the legal and logistical aspects of adoption, the adop-tion specialists would understand the importance of providing counsel and advocacy for their clients and would add a level of oversight that should be reassuring to the CPS caseworkers as well as to the birth and adoptive parents.

In a case like Maddie's, where everything happened in a rush, the involvement of an adoption specialist in addition to the CPS worker wouldn't have saved more than a few hours' time, but it would have eliminated an enormous amount of stress for all parties. In most cases, the goal would be to involve the adoption specialist prior to the birth of the baby so that the parents can make realistic plans about adoption. Too often, even though CPS already knows these clients and their limited options, the official decision to relinquish is made in a flurry of activity after the birth and under threat of having the baby placed in foster care if the birth parents don't follow through with the adoption. While that may be the sad reality of the situation, these prospective birth parents still deserve the counsel and advice about adoption that an adoption specialist can provide.

In addition to meeting the needs of parents who wish or need to plan an adoption, the timely involvement of an adoption specialist could save a great deal of time and money for DCYF by preventing unnecessary legal procedures and foster care placements. Creating a system in which state child welfare workers and adoption professionals could work together collaboratively instead of competitively would benefit everyone, including the taxpayers.

CHAPTER SIXTEEN

~

Not to Scare You, But . . .

I've been an adoption counselor for a very long time, but I still worry about inadvertently doing something that will get me or one of my clients into trouble. This is not because I am engaging in or encouraging risky behavior but because the definition of what is risky and what isn't can be very hard to pin down. There have been times when the press has condemned "errant" adoption professionals or adoptive families who have gotten into difficulty, and I've thought, "That could have been me." In fact, on one occasion it *was* me, and I feel lucky that there haven't been more occasions like that because trouble can sometimes be very hard to recognize and avoid, for both adoption professionals and for adoptive families.

My particular crime—for which I was named in a lawsuit charging me with racketeering and kidnapping—was to complete a home study for a family who had the misfortune of having a father change his mind about relinquishment after the placement of the baby. His charge was that the mother had deliberately given birth in a state with less stringent laws about the rights of fathers in order to subvert their ability to prevent an adoption. The mother maintained that she had traveled to that state to be with supportive relatives. Unfortunately for the father, he had signed the relinquishment papers and hadn't registered his objection until after the baby had been legally placed in an adoptive home, and the adoption was ultimately upheld. Unfortunately for the adoptive family, this period of contention was enormously stressful and expensive. All confidentiality had been breached, and the birth father continued to harass the family with requests for financial compensation.

Although his anger was initially directed at the mother and her attorney, the adoptive parents were the ones who suffered the most as a result of this man's change of heart, despite the fact that they had done nothing wrong. They—and I, who had never even spoken with the birth mother—had no input into or control over where she had decided to give birth.

Fortunately, these adoptive parents are extremely wise and ethical people, and they had a loving and supportive network of family and friends to help them through this time. But they must be dreading the day they'll need to talk with their son about what happened. And they must be further dreading the thought that someday he is likely to hear his birth father's version of the story, which includes his belief that the boy's adoptive parents were (like me) guilty of racketeering and kidnapping. Although these parents initially embraced the concept of open adoption, it is hard to imagine that any sort of comfortable relationship with their child's birth father will be possible after all the acrimony.

Not to scare you, but if this sort of thing can happen to that family, and to this adoption specialist, it can happen to anyone.

Adoption law and practice varies widely from state to state and sometimes even from courtroom to courtroom. This lack of national standardization leaves everyone vulnerable and tempts people to do exactly what that birth father was accusing the birth mother and me of doing: seeking out certain "adoption friendly" states that are less apt to respect a father's rights. In most states it is necessary to obtain the father's consent in order to place a baby in an adoptive home. If the father objects to the adoption, he will prevail in nearly all cases. All states recognize and uphold the rights of a father who wishes to parent his child, and neither parent has the right to force the other to relinquish their rights in order to facilitate an adoption.

But things get complicated when the father's whereabouts (and perhaps even his identity) are unknown, or when he is unresponsive or unwilling to communicate with the mother or her attorney. In these cases, his lack of involvement creates a period of stress and uncertainty for the mother and the adoptive parents. It also creates the need for expensive legal action: first to publish a legal notice for the father and then to terminate his parental rights. In an effort to avoid these problems and to assign some responsibility to the father, many states have created what is known as a putative father registry, where men can make known their wish to retain parental rights to any children they might father. Men who believe that an adoption might be planned without their knowledge or consent simply need to put their names on this registry, which attorneys must check to make sure there is no objection to an adoption from the father. It's simple and logical, and it seems to work, but there are still a number of states that operate without a putative father registry.

It is unfortunately true that some women who are planning an adoption do choose to "simplify" the legal process by arranging for the birth to happen in an adoption-friendly state. And it is true that there are "adoption professionals" who will help them succeed at this endeavor. But any effort to sidestep the father's rights in this way is extremely risky and unethical and leaves the child and the adoptive family vulnerable to the possibility of having the adoption overturned.

I don't know whether the mother in my "racketeering and kidnapping" case gave birth in another state in order to thwart the father. I don't really know anything at all about that particular woman. But I do know there are adoption professionals who take advantage of adoption-friendly states.

Here's how that worked for one of them. For about a ten-year period I would occasionally get calls from unhappy pregnant women currently living in a small town in Utah, then considered an adoption-friendly state. The women were usually from one of several southern states but had moved to Utah to take advantage of an offer to pay all their living expenses and connect them to their choice of an adoptive family. The women (sometimes along with their young children) were given bus tickets for the trip and set up in an apartment when they arrived. A counselor would visit periodically and take them to the store and to their medical appointments, but they were mostly left on their own. They were expected to wait patiently and safely until they gave birth.

But some of these women became unhappy when things in Utah were not what they had expected. They reported that the apartments were in areas where they felt isolated, lonely, and controlled. They felt they had no ability to make decisions or act independently. Of most concern to many of the women was the fact that they felt they had been misled about their choice of adoptive families. Only after arriving in the state did they realize (or acknowledge) that all the families the agency worked with were of the same religion, and it was not one they wanted to choose for their child.

In addition to being generally unhappy, some of these women were confused about their obligation to follow through with an adoption after having accepted money. They believed that if they didn't choose one of the families the agency represented, they would have to pay back the money it had spent on them, a misconception some of the agencies not only implied but flatly stated. (This all took place before paying for living expenses had become common practice.) Angry and scared, some of the women began calling other adoption professionals, like myself, in hopes that we could rescue them. But all I could do when they called me was to remind them that they were free to leave (not really useful information for someone with no traveling money) and refer them to one of the attorneys I work with. This attorney provided them with good legal advice and went on to make a valiant effort to regulate the practice of bringing pregnant women into Utah for the purpose of taking advantage of adoption-friendly laws designed to get around the laws in the women's home states.

These two stories illustrate how easy it is, both ethically and legally, to get into trouble. I have just told you about a case in which pregnant women were basically being deceived and trafficked by an agency that intended to ignore whatever the laws were in the state where they lived, along with the rights of the fathers of their babies. The Utah agency, and others like it that engaged in bald ethical violations, were allowed to operate unimpeded, whereas the adoptive family I worked with, engaging in what was ultimately deemed completely legal and ethical adoption practice, ended up in a protracted and expensive legal battle.

In 2015 Reid and Ben (the fathers of Logan and Carter in chapter 12) unknowingly worked with an agency that was engaged in bringing pregnant women into their state to take advantage of adoption-friendly laws. They worked with this agency for their first adoption and discovered only after Logan was placed with them that there was a problem with the way it operated. Fortunately for Reid and Ben and Logan, their own adoption wasn't in jeopardy, but other families weren't as lucky. The agency lost its license, and most of the families then working with the agency lost whatever part of the agency fee they had already paid. Some waiting adoptive families were able to maintain their connection to the pregnant women who had chosen them, but because the agency was now closing, they had to come up with more money to hire attorneys to complete their adoptions.

So how can adoptive families protect themselves?

You know how the number-one rule of real estate is "location, location, location"? The number-one rule of adoption should be "attorney, attorney, attorney." The only family I've ever worked with that actually had their adoption overturned was guilty only of making the understandable mistake of hiring an attorney who was a family friend rather than an expert in adoption. In their situation the birth mother, who was the daughter of an acquaintance, had approached them about adopting her baby. The family hired me to do the home study and postplacement report, and everything appeared to be going well for a few months after the baby was placed with the family. But the birth mother, who was at that time living in a car with her older boyfriend, began asking the adoptive family for money. They tried to talk to her about the wisdom of going back home, but she wasn't interested in doing that. The adoptive parents agreed to help her out financially for a few months but finally had to tell her they couldn't continue to do so. A short time later they, and I, were contacted by an attorney the birth mother had hired to overturn the adoption and get her baby back.

At first I wasn't overly concerned, since both birth parents had signed consents and the adoption had been finalized. It didn't appear that there were any grounds for objection. In my own conversations with the new attorney, I found him to be aggressive, bordering on threatening, and he seemed focused on proving that the birth mother had somehow been tricked into relinquishing her child. I felt some concern about the fact that the family had given her money (without getting court approval), but since that had been done after the legal placement of the baby, it didn't seem like it could be considered coercive. Once an adoption has been finalized, the courts have no further power to control what adoptive parents do with their money.

Some time passed before a court date was set, and my role in the process was simply to listen to the adoptive mom express her fears. It seemed inconceivable that the baby would be taken away from her adoptive parents, but in the end it turned out that the birth mother's attorney had uncovered a seemingly inconsequential error on the part of the adoptive parents' attorney and the judge had no choice but to overturn the adoption.

The family's attorney did not specialize in adoption, but as an old family friend, he offered to help them so they would save money on legal fees. On the day the birth parents' rights were terminated, the attorney arrived at court a few minutes early. A short time later he was summoned inside, and apparently neither he nor the presiding judge thought to check the clock to make sure that the required forty-eight hours had passed between the time the birth mother had signed her consent and the time the court terminated her parental rights. It turned out that they were a few minutes shy of the required forty-eight hours, and thus, technically speaking, the termination of her rights was invalid. The fact that the birth mother didn't make any effort to reclaim her child until months later, after the family declined to continue supporting her, turned out to be legally irrelevant.

The lesson to be learned from this story is not as terrifying as it seems because there is a way to protect against it. All the heartache this family experienced could have been avoided if they had used an attorney who specialized in adoption and who would have known the importance of scrupulous adherence to every single legal detail. Such an attorney would have known to wait the full forty-eight hours so that the adoption could never be overturned on this technicality. I imagine the family's attorney still beats himself up for his error, and the judge should be held equally responsible for the undoing of this adoption. The family ended up with a substantial settlement from the attorney's malpractice insurance, which in no way compensated for their loss. But I suspect that even they don't entirely blame him. Adoption law is complicated and the stakes of making an error are incredibly high—in fact life-changing. I've used this family's story many times over the years to illustrate the importance of using an experienced adoption attorney, and to let people know that this is one aspect of adoption over which they have complete control.

My second rule of adoption would be "counselor, counselor, counselor," and I would clarify that to mean "experienced adoption counselor." Even experienced adoption counselors are by no means infallible in protecting their clients from troubles, but they can help. I think it's safe to say that the most valuable service I provide these days is being available for the phone calls from families who want some quick input from me. Often these families have been contacted by an adoption professional who has seen their online profile and is representing a pregnant women who is considering adoption. The family has been given a little information about her and are now being asked to send money if they want their information to be presented so that this woman can consider them as parents for her baby.

With lots of experience fueling my cynicism, I usually want to tell people not to get involved, but I don't. Counselors aren't supposed to tell people what to do, and in truth, I don't want to be held responsible for their decisions. But I do want to help them figure out for themselves whether pursuing this sort of lead seems foolhardy, an acceptable risk, or possibly even an exciting leap of faith. And I try to help them reach an agreement with each other about how to proceed so that later there will be no opportunity for blame or guilt if things don't go well. Just as it is with attorneys who specialize in adoption, counselors who specialize in adoption have a specialized skill set that isn't readily accessible to other counselors, no matter how good they are at other types of counseling. A knowledgeable adoption counselor can make the difference between having a happy or a miserable adoption experience. And, as is true with hiring an experienced adoption attorney, having an experienced counselor on your team is another way adoptive families can take control of the process.

Perhaps the most important assistance a good attorney and a good counselor can give to adoptive parents is to help them maintain their emotional equilibrium through a process that seems designed to destroy it. Fortifying themselves with expertise is particularly important for families who are adopting privately or through an adoption facilitator. They can find themselves in situations that require snap decisions but provide little of the information they need to make them. Legal and ethical standards can vary from state to state, and although families cannot be expected to be knowledgeable about all these variations, they can still be held accountable for not being aware of them. Families who act without the advice of their attorney can find themselves in legal trouble they could not otherwise see coming.

The most common ethical quandary arises when pregnant women say they are in urgent need of financial assistance. This request might be from a woman who says she wants to plan an adoption for her baby. She is due in a month, but she has two other young children to take care of and is about to be evicted. If she doesn't give the landlord $300 immediately, he will put them on the streets.

Obviously, there is no guarantee that this woman is really about to be evicted, or has two other children, or is even actually pregnant, so is it worth $300 to take a chance on her? The family decides since the due date is only a month away, paying some of her living expenses would still be less expensive and less risky in the long run than if they had connected with a woman earlier in her pregnancy. They also tell themselves that, apart from the possibility of adopting her baby, it would feel better to them to meet the needs of this woman now than to save $300 even if they later discover that she is a scammer.

So they send the money. The woman is extremely grateful, and she and the hopeful adoptive mom have several nice phone conversations over the next few days. The family is reluctant to push her on the subject of adoption but does ask her to speak with their attorney. She agrees to do so and tells the attorney that she and the baby's father are no longer in communication, so she doesn't know how to locate him. The attorney explains to the family that they will need to publish a notice for the father, a lengthy and expensive process, and they agree to this additional expense and risk. The attorney arranges for the woman to meet with an attorney in the city where she lives, and the family sends a substantial fee to retain that attorney's services. A few days later the woman tells them that the landlord is now asking for the full rent, which is $1,200, and the family sends her the money. They have now spent a great deal of money without any assurance that this woman isn't scamming.

A couple of weeks pass, during which the prospective birth and adoptive mothers continue to talk on the phone. Though the pregnant woman doesn't directly ask for more money, it is evident that she could use it, and the hopeful adoptive mother feels bad when she ignores this hardship. Part of her feels terrible thinking about the other children's suffering and part of her feels terrible for wondering if the other children even exist. It is now only a week before the due date and the woman continues to say that she wants to follow through with an adoption. She says she missed the appointment with the attorney in her city because she couldn't find a babysitter, but another appointment has been scheduled. The due date is so soon that the couple book a flight and a hotel and arrange to take some time off work because they expect to need to stay in the other city for at least a week when the baby is born. They wait in a state of high excitement and anxiety for the phone to ring, summoning them to the birth of their child.

A week after the due date they are still waiting. The woman didn't show up for the second appointment with the attorney and hasn't responded to anyone's efforts to get in touch with her. She no longer answers her phone. Intellectually, the family knows that she is gone, and they are angry about having wasted all that money. But emotionally there is still a part of them that can't quite come to grips with what has happened, and it takes many months before their hearts stop generating flickers of hope each time the phone rings.

Very sadly, this family's story is not a horrifying exception to the rule. I've known many families who have experienced something similar, enduring emotional and financial suffering that can be much more protracted and extreme than what this family went through. In retrospect it seems easy to see that they should have known better or cut their losses earlier in the process, but the truth is that many successful adoptions start out looking very much like the ones that turn out to be scams. Even the most experienced attorneys and counselors can't always tell the difference, but they can definitely improve a family's odds of figuring it out.

CHAPTER SEVENTEEN

~

Adoption Specialists

When I was a sophomore in college, I applied for a job as a resident aide. One of the interview questions was, "What would you do if someone came to you for advice about how to handle an unplanned pregnancy?" Abortion had not yet been legalized. I responded that I felt that talking to a counselor (rather than a student RA) might be a good idea and could tell instantly that I was coming across as judgmental, as if I thought anyone with an unplanned pregnancy needed to see a therapist. I couldn't really explain what I meant (and I didn't get the job) but I have had a whole career's worth of time to fine-tune my answer and to figure out how important it is not to be judgmental.

All these years later, I realize that what I wanted to say was that I felt that a college student facing the decisions necessitated by an unplanned pregnancy deserved a more knowledgeable ear than that of a peer. I imagined that a well-informed and supportive advocate would be helpful in making the life-altering decisions the situation required.

The sort of supportive advocate I had in mind might be called an adoption specialist rather than an adoption counselor or an adoption advocate. Semantics are important here, and I don't want there to be any suggestion that women who are considering adoption are necessarily in need of counseling or therapy. Nor should there be any suggestion that an adoption specialist is acting as an advocate for adoption. The adoption specialist's role would be to help women who have expressed an interest in knowing more about adoption explore all their options, including parenting, and, when appropriate, to assist them in deciding if and how they want to proceed with an adoption. An adoption specialist would provide information to ensure that women are fully informed and are not being pressured or coerced, emotionally or financially, into making any particular decision.

I believe that any woman planning an adoption for her child should be required to have at least one meeting with an adoption specialist, much like meeting with an attorney is now part of planning an adoption. Some women might decide after the meeting that this sort of assistance is not of value to them and decline any further contact, but they would at least have been provided with the opportunity to obtain unbiased information. Not only would the practice of requiring a meeting with an adoption specialist help to uncover evidence of coercion, it could also help determine whether the woman had serious doubts about, or even no intention of, following through with an adoption. Making these discoveries early in the process will save time and heartache for both birth and adoptive parents. Women who do not choose adoption could instead focus on decisions and plans regarding parenting. Prospective adoptive parents could save time and money on unnecessary legal fees and living expenses for adoptions that do not happen. Perhaps most importantly, meetings with an unbiased adoption specialist could help ensure that both the birth and adoptive parents had observed the highest ethical standards in planning the adoption.

There have been ongoing efforts to provide services similar to what I am calling for, and I have occasionally been asked to serve in such a capacity, but with one crucial difference: In each of the cases I was involved with, I was brought in at the eleventh hour to meet with a pregnant woman to "confirm her consent." Like my vision of the duties of an adoption specialist, the purpose of having a counselor confirm consent is to make sure that the woman is acting of her own free will. However, in my case, it was always clear to me that any difficulty I might uncover would not be welcomed. No matter how ethical the adoptive parents and their attorney might be, they weren't really asking that I step in and impartially explore options with the expectant mother. What they wanted and expected me to do was supply an extra stamp of approval on the adoption.

There were times at meetings like these when it became obvious that the birth and adoptive parents had wildly different ideas about what the adoption would look like. I remember a situation in which a pregnant girl talked excitedly about the upcoming eighteen years and her anticipation of all-expenses-paid trips to California, where she would stay in the adoptive parents' home and enjoy the company of the child to whom she was about to give birth. The adoptive parents didn't share this vision, but they weren't going to say so and risk angering the girl two weeks before her due date. This particular girl seemed so immature to me that I feared her current decision to relinquish her baby might actually hinge on whether she felt she could look forward to those trips.

If ever a situation cried out for a counselor's involvement, it was this one, but there wasn't time to do much of anything to help, especially since the adoptive parents and the girl's parents seemed focused on getting an adoption accomplished with as little discussion and drama as possible. But that "fingers crossed; just don't rock the boat" approach seldom works. In the end, not surprisingly, the girl did not follow through with the adoption and the hopeful adoptive family spent a lot of money on legal fees and other expenses on an adoption that didn't happen.

I believe that if this young woman had been required to meet with an adoption specialist at some point earlier in the process, it would have quickly become evident that she had no concept of what it would mean to relinquish her baby. She did not have the maturity to understand the gravity of relinquishment. Meeting with an adoption specialist wouldn't have changed the outcome, but it could have helped everyone understand much sooner what that outcome was going to be and spared the hopeful adoptive parents much financial and emotional loss. It also could have helped the girl's parents come to terms with the reality of their daughter's decision and what the three of them needed to be doing to ensure her well-being and the well-being of the baby. Instead, everyone put blinders on, and mother and baby came home to a house filled with chaos and unhappiness.

It is not uncommon in situations in which other people are strongly promoting adoption (typically the baby's father, one or more of the grandparents, and/or the adoptive parents) for everyone to quite deliberately choose to stay in a state of denial throughout the pregnancy. They don't want the expectant mother to think too much about how hard it will be to relinquish the baby, and they fear that any discussion of alternatives to adoption will legitimize the idea that she might choose a different option. The mother herself often tends to believe that these people know what is best for her. But all this certainty can quickly evaporate with the birth of the baby if the "decision" to relinquish was rooted in denial and everyone has simply been avoiding the truth.

I sometimes hear statements like the following from young women or their parents to explain why adoption is the only possible choice: "I can't keep the baby; I'm not old enough" or "she can't keep the baby; she can't even take care of her cat" or "I've never been one of those people who was really into babies." While these may all be perfectly true and logical reasons for choosing adoption, they are almost never sufficient. When the baby arrives and the young woman finally allows some emotion into the equation, she begins to understand what relinquishment will really mean.

It is neither effective nor ethical to try to force a relinquishment for practical reasons. Practicalities will influence the decision to relinquish parental rights, but without an acknowledgment of the emotional complexities of what they are facing, women often cast aside practical reasons when the baby finally becomes real to them. The adoption specialist's job is to help the baby become real as early in the pregnancy as possible so that these important decisions can be based in reality rather than wishful thinking and can be made in a timely and well-thought-out manner. The involvement of an adoption specialist would not increase or decrease the likelihood of an adoption taking place. It would be aimed not at influencing a woman's decision about adoption but at influencing the timing of that decision and at saving everyone time, trouble, expense, and heartache.

One of the things I have learned over four decades working with women who have relinquished babies is that most of them would have been quite capable of raising those babies if their circumstances had been different. They were at a stage in their lives during which they believed they were unable to provide for a child in the manner they felt their baby deserved. They chose adoption in an effort to give their child the life they wanted him or her to have. These women loved their babies and acted in what they believed were their best interests. They sought the help of an adoption professional because they had a specific need for assistance in planning an adoption, and that was usually the only form of assistance they needed.

But there are also women seeking help planning an adoption who are coping with significant other problems, such as an abusive relationship with the father of the baby, an ongoing problem with substance abuse or mental illness, an insecure housing situation, and/or general financial stress. All these other concerns affect the well-being of women and their babies, and they influence decisions about adoption. While it is evident that women in these circumstances would benefit from assistance that speaks directly to these other concerns, that is not the sort of assistance an adoption specialist would provide directly. Instead, she would assist in connecting women to various service providers who can more effectively address these other specific areas of concern and provide appropriate resources. In addition to referrals for social support, the adoption specialist could help connect pregnant women who need financial assistance to sources of support that are independent of the adoption. This would have the clear advantages of eliminating any element of financial pressure to relinquish, eliminating the financial burden and risk to the adoptive parents, eliminating any incentive for scammers, and providing financial assistance to pregnant women that isn't going to automatically end shortly after the birth of the baby.

Of course, the success of a such a system using adoption specialists would depend on the individuals involved and their commitment to providing unbiased and ethical assistance. Adoption specialists must fully understand that they are not being asked to act as therapists or arbiters of morality who analyze or pass judgment on their clients. They must also understand that it would be unacceptable for them to attempt to influence the decisions their clients make about adoption. They cannot see into the future or into peoples' hearts, and they cannot know who will or won't become a good parent. Adoption specialists can, when necessary, make the appropriate referral to child protective services if they feel a child is in danger, but they also need to be able to recognize and understand that there are many parents in the world who are "good enough."

The success of an adoption specialist system would also rely on these specialists' ability to act independently of any individual who will directly benefit from an adoptive placement. Ideally, funding would be provided through an independent entity (either private or governmental), but the services of the adoption specialist could also be funded by prospective adoptive parents. Their interests, in turn, would be served if one of the first steps in the legal process was a relatively inexpensive meeting with an adoption specialist rather than a much more expensive meeting with an attorney.

I am often contacted by adoptive parents who are seeking advice about worrisome communications with prospective birth mothers. As I have mentioned, I believe that most adoptive parents want and value the sort of information and advice I and other adoption counselors can provide at these times. It is always in the adoptive parents' best interest to have an honest and objective assessment of the situation, perhaps especially so if the assessment indicates that there are problems that need attention. People tend to blame the messenger for bad news, and prospective adoptive parents are unlikely to feel grateful for unwelcome information, at least initially. But it isn't in anyone's best interest to run from the truth. If prospective birth and adoptive parents can communicate honestly with each other, they may be able to handle any problems that arise. If the problems are insurmountable, at least everyone can cut their losses sooner rather than later. It feels terrible to hopeful adoptive parents to lose a connection with a prospective birth mother during the pregnancy, but it does not feel as terrible as losing that connection after the baby has been born.

CHAPTER EIGHTEEN

~

Adoption Reform

I think the primary impediment to reforming the infant adoption system is society's lack of awareness that there really is a problem. There are occasionally scary stories in the media about ethical violations, but they are likely to be attributed to individual bad actors rather than a dysfunctional system. This is much the same as the way we want to blame a negligent caseworker when a child in foster care is harmed, rather than a child welfare system that assigns each caseworker responsibility for an impossibly large number of children. We like the idea of being able to fix the problem by getting rid of the caseworker instead of reforming an enormously complex child welfare system. But while the dysfunction in the adoption system is also complex, it isn't nearly as complex as the entire child welfare system, and it certainly shouldn't be viewed as unfixable.

Another impediment to reform is reluctance, and even outright refusal on the part of adoption professionals and adoptive parents, to acknowledge that the adoption process has become dysfunctional. As an adoption professional, I know I have found myself unhappily broadening the parameters of acceptable practice over the years, right along with everyone around me. If I hadn't, I would have been left far behind as all the baby brokers surged ahead. I've done a lot of commiserating with families about how bad things have gotten over the years, but I still function in that bad system. I understand that adoption profes-sionals need to be cooperative and diplomatic with one another, but I am urging them not to be complacent, not to "go along to get along," as I did for so many years, with what they know to be ethically questionable practices.

I am urging adoptive parents to voice their complaints. There is often quite a discrepancy between the degree of unhappiness they feel about the adoption process before they have their baby and their memories of that unhappiness after the baby arrives. This isn't surprising, and new parents certainly need and deserve to focus happily on their babies. But it is unfortunate that the lessons we could learn from their experi-ences simply vanish if adoptive parents don't express their concerns. I have frequently listened to a family's tale of woe about enduring clear violations of ethical standards and felt sure that heads would roll if the press got wind of their story. I have urged families in these situations to pursue a formal complaint in hopes of saving the next family from such abuse. But I can recall only a few times, over a long career, when a family has actually done so. I understand their reluctance to complain, since I have been guilty of silence as well. I haven't wanted to challenge or accuse any adoption professional who might one day assist one of the families I work with in finding a baby to adopt. I've played it safe for my own sake and for that of the families I care about. But now I believe that speaking out, rather than playing it safe, will better serve both birth and adoptive families.

Since this book has been devoted to exposing problems within the adoption system, some readers might conclude that I have an awfully pessimistic view of adoption. This is not the case. As both an adoptive parent and an adoption professional, I know that adoption provides, for most people, an overwhelmingly positive foundation of love and family. Although the process of creating an adoptive family has become increasingly difficult, I want to point out that all but one of the families whose stories I have told in this book were ultimately successful in their efforts to adopt a baby. It should also be noted that the unsuccessful family (Ben and Ellie, who were baby Ava's foster-to-adopt parents) would almost certainly have been able to adopt eventually had they kept trying. They didn't do so because they were emotionally drained by what they had gone through and could not risk another heartbreaking round of losses. Sadly, adoption is going to continue to be too painful for some families, and even with the best intentions, adoption professionals can't protect all of their clients from bad experiences. But we can do better than we have been doing. We can make changes that will improve the process of adoption for everyone.

I am by no means the first person to point out the need for improvement or to call for the specific changes I feel are necessary to restore or create ethical adoption practice. I find myself in good—and interestingly diverse—company in asking for adoption reform. I also find that there is a surprising and heartening level of agreement about what should be done, even among people who have primarily opposing views about the ethics of infant adoption.

A Google search on "adoption reform" eventually leads to the writings of two passionate and articulate individuals, one an adoptive parent and nationally respected spokesperson/advocate for adoption, and the other a woman who wholeheartedly believes that infant adoption is entirely corrupt and that, like her, all birth mothers come to regret the decision to relinquish their parental rights. You wouldn't expect them to share much common ground in their opinions, but some of the reforms they urge are essentially the same, and many are the changes I would call for as well.

The Establishment of Standards of Practice for Adoption Professionals

Every few years, an adoptive mother I have just worked with asks me how she can get into the adoption. It's always someone I've enjoyed working with, and I like to think that her interest reflects well on the connection that we've made. But I'm also a little dismayed. To begin with, none of these women are considering going back to school for training as a counselor, nor are they offering to volunteer at an adoption agency in order to get some experience in the field. They are assuming that they had learned all they needed to know simply from going through the process of adopting their own child.

What they want from me are tips about how the business works. The only one of these women who actually pursued adoption counseling had previously worked as a realtor, and she felt the same social skills that made her successful in that career would serve her just as well in the role of adoption counselor. She lasted not quite a year before realizing the job was more complicated and a lot less financially rewarding than she had expected.

The main reason I am dismayed, however, is that there isn't anything preventing people who have no credentials from declaring themselves adoption professionals. States have established require- ments for licensed counselors and agencies, but there are no similar licensing requirements for adoption facilitation services or for adoption consultants. These people may in fact have excellent credentials, but there is no requirement that they must, and it is sadly true that there are many people who present themselves as adoption professionals who do not have adequate education or experience.

Working with prospective birth and adoptive parents is a sensitive and complicated undertaking, and an uninformed approach to one's clients is not only unhelpful but can be hugely damaging. Adoption professionals work with people at a vulnerable time in their lives, when the consequences of the decisions they are making are life-altering. It is dismaying to know that many birth and adoptive parents place their trust in people who have received no formal training and are not sub- ject to any sort of regulation or oversight.

This needs to change. We need to establish basic licensing standards for anyone who is paid to provide adoption services, whether they call themselves counselors, facilitators, consultants, advocates, matchers, or anything else. If they provide any sort of service to birth or adoptive parents, they should be required to prove that they have the necessary skills.

The Establishment of Methods of Oversight and Review of Adoption Professionals

Adoptive parents are advised that they must exercise all due diligence in choosing which adoption professionals to work with. But they soon find that there is little information available to help them in what turns out to be an elusive task. At present, people have to rely primarily on chat rooms and online reviews, both of which can be tremendously misleading. Online reviews are by nature subjective, and reviewers (aside from the ones who have been specifically asked to write positive reviews) are more likely to be people who feel the need to air a grievance than those sharing stories of satisfaction. Chat rooms may be a bit more balanced, but many are likely to be dominated by people who have strong opinions that may or may not be factual or relevant to another person's situation. We need a reliable and respected process for review.

We also need to establish a reliable process for oversight of adoption professionals. Adoption agencies and licensed counselors are subject to state regulation and oversight; if they fail to maintain certain standards, including ongoing formal education, they risk losing their license. However, adoption facilitators, consultants, and other unlicensed workers are not held to the same standard. And there is no established procedure for fielding the complaints of pregnant women or adoptive families who believe they have been mistreated. Short of taking legal action, contacting the press, or venting online, victims of unethical or incompetent practices have no recourse.

Even in truly egregious cases, which have resulted in lawsuits and media attention, the offending individuals are often able to escape censure and continue working unimpeded. Since they are not required to be licensed, they are also not required to uphold any standards necessary for licensing. Offenses that would result in a loss of license for a licensed adoption professional do not have the same impact on unlicensed adoption professionals unless they rise to an actionable level and the aggrieved party chooses to pursue legal action. The question is, whose interests are being served by the absence of licensing requirements? Certainly not those of the pregnant women and adoptive parents, who are led to believe that they are working with individuals who will be held accountable for providing professional service.

The Establishment of National Adoption Laws and Regulations

A national standard of adoption laws and best practices should be established, and anyone professionally involved with an adoption should be held accountable for meeting this national standard. There would be no variation from state to state, and consequently no incentive to evade the law by seeking out "adoption-friendly" states. A national standard would eliminate confusion and the expectation that adoptive parents can be held legally accountable for knowing the intricacies of adoption laws in all fifty states. Since a national standard would simplify the legal process, it would therefore also serve to lower attorney fees and reduce the stress of adoption by making the legal process less opaque and ambiguous.

The Establishment of a System of Cooperation Rather Than Competition between the State Child Welfare System and the Private Adoption System

The adoption spokesperson mentioned earlier and I both call for reform that encourages, if not mandates, coordination between the state departments of social and health services and licensed adoption professionals.

The foster care system struggles to meet the needs of the children in its care despite ongoing, diligent, and heartfelt efforts at reform. We need to recognize that reuniting children with their birth families isn't always a realistic goal and that adoption is a viable option for parents who are not capable of changing the negligent or abusive behavior toward their children that resulted in the foster care placement in the first place. And we need to accomplish this in a timely manner. There is no excuse for allowing children to spend years in foster care while their parents fail to make the changes necessary to become safe caretakers and regain custody. We also need to recognize that there are some parents who are not motivated to change their behavior and would choose adoption for their children if they could do so in a manner less adversarial than a courtroom battle to terminate their parental rights.

The idea that the foster care and adoption systems could coordinate their efforts is explored more fully in my previous book, *The Children Money Can Buy*, which describes my own experiences working in both the foster care and the adoption systems. In both cases, an attitude of mutual distrust prevailed. It won't be easy to inspire cooperation, but we could at least start with the assumption that we are all trying to accomplish the goal of making life better for the children in our care. In some cases foster care will be better at doing that, and in other cases adoption will.

The Establishment of a National Policy Prohibiting Prospective Adoptive Parents from Providing Payment for Living Expenses to Prospective Birth Parents

Somewhat surprisingly, it was not the adoption spokesperson but the woman who had relinquished a baby who called for reform in the practice that I feel has had the single biggest impact on the erosion of ethical standards in adoption. Although I do not agree with her general negativity about adoption, this woman and I agree that the exchange of money corrupts the adoption process.

I have witnessed the payment of living expenses negatively impacting adoption in the following ways:

1. By exerting financial pressure on pregnant women to consider and/or follow through with an adoption
2. By pressuring pregnant women to merely pretend to consider adoption
3. By encouraging women to become pregnant in order to receive financial support
4. By creating dysfunctional financial liaisons between adoption professionals and women who pursue multiple pregnancies and relinquishments
5. By increasing the number of adoption scams
6. By dramatically increasing the overall cost of adoption, including unsuccessful adoptions
7. By eroding trust and goodwill between birth and adoptive parents

I expect that people are going to accuse me of being hard-hearted and unrealistic in calling for the elimination of payments for birth mother living expenses. I want to make it clear that I am fully in support of financial assistance for pregnant women, along with others in need, but I feel that when assistance is necessary, it should come from the government or some other neutral source rather than from individual adoptive parents.

The last thing I want this book to do is give people the impression that all pregnant women who accept living expenses are acting in a coldhearted or manipulative manner. Nor do I want to give the impression that adoptive parents who find themselves competing financially with one another are being calculating or manipulative. All of them are simply acting in ways that they believe are in their own, and ultimately the child's, best interest. And despite what I've had to say about some of them, adoption professionals are almost always doing their best too. But we all need to do better.

CHAPTER NINETEEN

~

Closing the Gray Market

This book will probably make a lot of people angry. It will certainly anger those I have accused of acting unethically, including agencies, attorneys, facilitators, and consultants who provide inadequate or biased "counseling" and exploit both birth and adoptive parents for their own financial gain. Although these people may have a very hard time recognizing themselves, the book will still make them uncomfortable. The book will also certainly anger the women I have accused of being repeat birth mothers (and the "adoption professionals" who exploit them), using their pregnancies and babies as a way to support themselves. Fortunately, the number of such women is small, but unless we do something to prevent it, it will undoubtedly grow.

Another group of people who will be unhappy with this book are birth and adoptive parents who feel accused of having taken part in a financial transaction. Some birth parents will protest, quite truthfully, that they were desperate and had no other choice. Others will protest the unfairness of a system in which the adoption professionals receive financial compensation while pregnant women are expected to righteously reject the very idea of being financially supported through their pregnancies. Adoptive parents will protest, also quite truthfully, that they had no option other than to agree to pay living expenses and/ or that they feel perfectly happy to have provided financial support for the birth parents of their child, though none will feel this way about having financially supported scammers.

My purpose in writing this book is not to lay blame on any individuals or even on any of the agencies and facilitators I have characterized as exploitative. While I believe that these people and entities are acting unethically, they are usually acting within the law, so the blame for their actions lies with our society's apparent lack of interest in more careful regulation of the adoption process. But the truth is that I *do* want this book to make people angry—angry enough to start asking tough questions about why the current approach to infant adoption seems necessary and why we seem uninterested in making improvements.

Yes, I want people to be angry. I hope that all the adoptive parents forced to take on unreasonable financial and emotional risks/burdens will be angry. I hope that birth mothers will be angry when they realize how much they have been controlled and how severely their babies' options have been limited by a system that was supposedly designed to help them. I hope that both birth and adoptive parents who have been denied the care and compassion that their situations demanded while the "professionals" left everything up to the laws of the marketplace will be angry. I want adoption professionals who have felt frustrated about working in an ethically compromised system to be angry. I want this book to make all these people so angry that they will feel energized, empowered, and compelled to demand change.

In an ideal world, children wouldn't need adoptive families and parents wouldn't need to adopt in order to parent children. But in the real world, some of these children and parents will find each other through adoption and create their own version of ideal. Adoption stories have been with us throughout history, and at their most basic they manifest an adaptive instinct to take care of the young and thereby ensure the survival of the species. Although there has been much criticism of adoption practice in recent years, the fact remains that it is essential to meeting the needs of many children. No matter how valid the objections to unethical practices in both domestic and international adoption, it is still the best way to ensure that we do indeed take care of some of our most imperiled young.

Most adoptive parents understand a couple of hard truths about adoption. First, our joy in parenthood is made possible by the sadness of our children's birth parents. Second, the enormity of the gift we have received is a debt that can be repaid only by a lifetime of love and care. Nothing less is sufficient. I believe adoptive parenthood comes with an extra responsibility as well—one that we owe to all members of the adoption triad, ourselves included—and that is to create an atmosphere in which respect and understanding can flourish and children can know that both their birth and adoptive parents' actions really were guided by love and the belief that adoption was in their best interest. We need an adoption system that can live up to that ideal.

~

Epilogue

Here's an update on a few people.

Owen and Kira

Being new parents was a little harder than Owen and Kira had expected because Jack was fussy, especially in the evenings. He also woke every three hours and took quite a while to get back to sleep after his nighttime feedings. Since Owen was the one who had to get up and go to work in the mornings, Kira let him sleep while she got up with the baby. After a few months, Jack's fussiness improved dramatically, and he started waking only once at night. But instead of feeling more rested, Kira was feeling exhausted. Her mother came over during the day to give her a chance to nap, and Kira would immediately fall into a deep sleep and wake up feeling groggy and disoriented. When Owen got home in the evenings he would sometimes find Kira sleeping on the floor next to Jack. She was afraid to hold him while sitting or lying on the couch for fear that she would fall asleep and roll on him or he would slip out of her arms. Even when Owen took over nighttime feedings on the weekends, Kira still couldn't seem to get enough rest. At the baby's four-month checkup, when the pediatrician asked Kira how she was doing, she burst into tears. It's not out of the ordinary for new mothers to feel overwhelmed, but Kira's reaction was so out of character that she and Owen decided something must be really wrong and she scheduled an appointment with her doctor. That's when they discovered Kira was almost three months pregnant.

This was definitely not what Owen and Kira had planned, but they were overjoyed. It looked like they would have their two children a couple months before they turned forty after all, but their kids would be less than a year instead of three years apart in age. Kira had a difficult pregnancy and stopped working after the first trimester. Without her income, she and Owen and Jack couldn't afford to continue living in their home. Rather than sell it, they made the decision to move back in with Kira's parents and rent their house to someone else. The rent they charged on their house barely covered their mortgage payments, but at least they could look forward to getting back into the house at some point in the future. Meanwhile, it was a godsend to have Kira's parents' help with Jack, then with the new baby: a girl they named Laine.

Owen and Kira feel immensely blessed to have two happy, healthy children, and they are fully appreciative of how fortunate they are to have so much support from the extended family. With lots of assistance, they were able to manage everything. Living with Kira's parents allowed them to save a big part of their income every month, but they still had to give up on their dream of having Kira stay home when the children were young. She went back to teaching when Laine was three months old, and although she always loved teaching, it was very hard for her to be away from the babies. The fact that they were with doting grandparents made it bearable.

Owen and Kira were able to move back into their home the year before Jack started kindergarten. They're still struggling financially and have realized that it will be at least another ten years before they will finally be completely free of their medical and adoption-related debt. Fortunately, Kira was eventually able to get a teaching job in the district where Owen works, so they now both have short commutes and more time with the children. Sharing a home with Kira's parents for almost five years was stressful for everyone, but it also facilitated especially close relationships between Jack and Laine and their grandparents.

Owen and Kira made it through everything on the strength of their relationship with each other and their extended families. Rather than feeling resentful, they are able to look back with pride and appreciation for having weathered all the difficult times, but they do feel discouraged about their financial future. Although they can't help but wish things had been easier, if everything had gone according to their original plan, they wouldn't be Jack or Laine's parents. So Owen and Kira feel enormously blessed.

Lindy

Lindy did not follow through with a fourth pregnancy and relinquishment. Instead she found the courage to schedule an appointment with the counselor she'd seen earlier who had helped her decide to return to school. At their first session, Lindy was able to summon up even more courage and tell the counselor what she had been thinking of doing. After a stunned and prolonged silence, the counselor discarded all effort to be professionally nondirective and told Lindy in no uncertain terms that another pregnancy would be a huge mistake. The counselor then took her personal involvement a step further and connected Lindy with a friend who was the director of nursing at a rehabilitation center. That woman offered Lindy a job and, eight months later, helped her obtain a scholarship and then enter a work-training program at a large hospital.

Things went smoothly after that, and Lindy eventually became a registered nurse. As she began to experience success in her training, Lindy also began to experience success in her interpersonal relationships. Her intelligence, diligence, and calm demeanor were all assets in her work and earned her the appreciation of her patients and the respect of her peers. Lindy was able to make real friends, a few of whom know about the babies and have offered compassion and understanding. She has not exactly put the past behind her, but Lindy is also coming to understand the girl she was and how little control she had over the circumstances that conspired against her. Lindy's most fervent wish is that someday her three children will also be able to understand that girl.

Julia

Two years later, Julia is still searching for her third child. She is reconsidering her decision not to work with the state foster care system.

John and Hannah

John and Hannah and Luca and Ariana are a very happy family, and both children are thriving in every respect. Like Owen and Kira, John and Hannah look back at all they went through with pride and gratitude, along with some very painful and complicated emotions. Although Hannah knows her children's adoptions are secure now, she sometimes can't help dwelling on the thought that things could have gone very differently for them. Most of the time her family seems like a fated miracle, but there are also times when Hannah fears they might all still be vulnerable. At those times she feels fragile as a parent and unsure about her ability to protect her children from unpredictable dangers. All the logical reassurance she gives herself can't simply erase the years of fear and insecurity that played such a huge part in the creation of her family.

Hannah doesn't talk about these feelings with John, afraid it would somehow tempt fate even to give voice to them. She does wonder if he has fears of his own, though, and is equally afraid to acknowledge them to her. Someday, she hopes, the fears will fade away and there will be no need to torture herself with thoughts about what could have happened if Luca and Ariana hadn't been allowed to become their children after all.

Ben and Ellie

Ben and Ellie did not ever become parents. Their story took place years ago, and although I believe there have been improvements in the foster-to-adopt process since then, it remains a necessarily risky undertaking for potential adoptive parents.

The stories of these eight people, heartrending and arduous though they are, are no more so than the stories of many of the other people

I work with. Most of them have stories that end with successful adoptions, and with gratitude for that fact. However, I believe that instead of looking back with satisfaction and pride, there are too many adoptive parents these days who are looking back in dismay and disbelief at having had to make their way through such a troubled and grueling process. They would absolutely go through it all again to end up with the children they have, but they can't help wondering why becoming parents had to be so hard.

It's much harder to categorize the stories of Lindy and other birth mothers by saying that they "ended in successful adoptions." Obviously, the situation is far too complicated to be summed up in this manner. Although Lindy voluntarily, seemingly even eagerly, relinquished her parental rights to each of the babies she gave birth to, these actions don't begin to explain her true story.

Lindy is not one particular person. Her story is a composite of several young women I worked with, and tragically, there are enormous numbers of girls like her who suffer childhoods of dysfunction and abuse and then go on to adult relationships that are similarly dysfunctional and abusive. Although she went through an especially painful period in her life, Lindy ultimately became an exception to a pattern in which girls who have been victimized throughout childhood find themselves tragically repeating that pattern throughout their adult lives and relationships.

My plea is for reform that will not put the adoption process and adoptive parents in the position of further victimizing these women.

Index

~

About the Author

Anne Moody is the codirector of an agency specializing in infant adoption. She is the author of *The Children Money Can Buy: Stories from the Frontlines of Foster Care and Adoption*, published in 2018 by Rowman & Littlefield. She is also an adoptive parent, and both her professional and personal background inform her work as an adoption specialist who advises clients on all aspects of the adoption experience.

CPSIA information can be obtained
at www.ICGtesting.com
Printed in the USA
BVHW041019020223
657586BV00003B/3

9 781538 174715